THE GRAND OLD MAN:
AMOS ALONZO STAGG

BY

JOHN GREENBURG

Best wishes John Greenburg

GRAPHIC DESIGN BY NELJO LLC

I would prefer to lose every game than win even one unfairly.

-- Amos Alonzo Stagg

America loves its Super Bowls. Every year, they're celebrated like a second New Year's Eve. Most of the people who watch this popular annual contest have no idea who Amos Alonzo Stagg was or what he possibly could have to do with the Super Bowl. Some may know that the University of Chicago's stadium, Stagg Field, was named after him; but few people know that neither the Super Bowl, nor football itself, would be the same exciting game we know and love today without him.

Can you imagine football without those thrilling passes -- the suspenseful "Hail Marys" and the gut-grabbing interceptions? The most sensational moments in football -- the moments every fan waits for, ready to add them to their mental scrapbook of favorite images and re-view them time and again -- these are due to the life's work of one man: Amos Alonzo Stagg. Although he died before the first Super Bowl was played, he gave us football's passing game and all the wonderful memories that came with it.

Some of the biggest names in football all agree on one thing: All football came from Stagg. They may have been referring to his fathering of football's forward pass, but Amos Alonzo Stagg was the Grand Old Man of football for so many reasons. He earned every possible honor and accolade. He was still coaching at the amazing age of 98, and his long life spanned the greater part of football's history. He helped shape the form that football was to take by playing a crucial role in its development; from its rudimentary beginnings to the sophisticated strategies of today. In fact, the story of his life in football could very well tell the story of the game of football itself.

There were once plans to make a movie of the life of Amos Alonzo Stagg and his wife, Stella; with Spencer Tracy and Katherine Hepburn in the starring roles. His inspirational story was a natural choice to be immortalized in film, and it would have given him his rightful place in our popular culture. It is unfortunate for all of us that the movie was never made.

The Grand Old Man himself tried to write the script, but found he couldn't complete the task. He once told one of his former players that he and Stella didn't want the story of their lives told until after their deaths. I believe he didn't finish his story because he couldn't envision its ending. After all, it was his motto in life, as well as football, to everlastingly fight the good fight. What he wanted most to do in his life was to pass on his hard-won knowledge about what it means to live a good life, and how dignity and respect flow from constant striving and unflagging faith. With Christian ideals to guide him, he forged a template for younger generations to follow. For him, coaching football became the best way to teach young men about the qualities that lead to success in any field of endeavor: Discipline, cooperation, fairness and perseverance.

I hope this book will do justice to this exceptional man.

John Greenburg
December 5, 2000

THE MAKING OF A GRAND MAN

Springtime had come to the San Joaquin Valley, but Amos Alonzo Stagg was in the winter of his years. The people of Stockton had grown familiar with the sight of the 92-year-old man going through his morning exercise rituals: Chin-ups on a branch of the large fig tree in his backyard, then a jog along the small course he set out among the trees. They could tell you how he had played a good game of tennis in his sixties, and ran a mile every day even into his eighties. They could even tell you how his life insurance company had to pay him for outliving the terms of his policy! After ninety-two years, he had some health problems -- a cataract in his left eye and the beginnings of Parkinson's Disease -- but he didn't trouble anyone with these and didn't allow himself to focus on them. He liked to concentrate on his activities because he had learned long ago about the satisfaction he felt in working hard and his pleasure in a good struggle.

After finishing his constitutional, he was ready to make it a good day. Concentration and a degree of struggle were required for what was in store for him, for he had made a commitment to putting his story into permanent form. He would keep at it for as long as it took. He may have been well-advanced in years, but the end was still not in sight.

As he sat at his desk, took out a blank sheet of paper and touched the point of his pen to it; the only question was where to start. Mr. Stagg chose to begin at the very beginning ... and so it will be.

Amos Alonzo Stagg was born August 16, 1862 in the New Jersey house his father, Amos Lindsley Stagg, had built with his own hands in 1848. Amos Lindsley was the great-grandson of John Stagg, Jr., who had served as General Washington's aide-de-camp at Valley Forge. Even with this proud lineage, his large family lacked financial means, so Amos Lindsley was unable to receive a formal education and, instead, was apprenticed to a shoemaker at the age of seven. Yet, he was an intelligent and ambitious young man and he taught himself to read. He read voraciously, becoming knowledgeable about American as well as world history, and he shared his passion for learning with his children, both sons and daughters.

When he was twenty-eight, he married Eunice Pierson, a descendant of the men who, back in 1666, purchased land from the Indians that eventually became Newark, New Jersey. Eunice was a petite woman, weighing only eighty pounds, but she was healthy and strong, and capably managed all the arduous tasks of the housework of that time. Together, husband and wife were models of industrious energy, and were respected members of their community of West Orange, New Jersey, with Amos Lindsley taking an active part in public affairs. In his unpublished work, Amos Alonzo wrote, "My mother had a sweet and gentle disposition and she was devoted to the interests of her children. My father was a hard worker and frugal, and succeeded in attending to all our physical needs, although for a number of years it was difficult to keep the wolf from our door. He earned his livelihood by cobbling and making shoes in the winter and by farming in the fertile months, as well as by doing all manners of odd jobs -- all the while keeping his children in school. None of us was taken out of school before the age of fourteen, which was common in those times. He seemed to take a special pleasure in instructing his own children, and he kept a watchful eye on our progress. It was under such fostering care that I grew to manhood pure in mind, with no bad habits."

Amos Lindsley and Eunice had eight children, three sons and five daughters, and Amos Alonzo was the sixth child born to them. From the time they were old enough, they were expected to contribute to the family's welfare by helping their parents whenever possible. Amos Alonzo proudly recalled, "While still quite young, I was able to plant and tend a garden, and by the age of fifteen, I helped my father in all kinds of farm work -- harvesting with a scythe and cradling wheat, oats and rye."

There were always chores to be done, but the Stagg children were allowed enough time for carefree play. Their cottage was surrounded by wooded slopes which were their playgrounds, and they played games like tree tag, shinny and something they called "raggedy mole", a version of hare and hounds. In the winter, there was skating and coasting, and the children skated on a big pond that later became the site of Thomas Edison's West Orange, New Jersey factory. Not too far away there was a swift-running stream of cold water that came from Orange Mountain, and at various places this stream was dammed to create Edenic watering holes. People came from as far as New York City to drink the fortifying waters of the famous Hutton Springs.

Even as a boy, Amos Alonzo was naturally athletic and enjoyed all kinds of sports, but what delighted him most was running. Whether racing or chasing or just breaking into a sprint, he loved to run. He had a passion for all the running games, especially baseball. He wrote that, "From my earliest remembrance, I had always played baseball. It took us kids many months to earn the $1.25 needed to buy a baseball. I was the treasurer of our club, which we called the Green Leaves, and I contributed my share by making and selling kites for one or two cents each."

In 1875, when Amos Alonzo was thirteen, he watched a professional baseball game between the New York Mutuals and the Orange, New Jersey team through a knothole in the fence behind the catcher. After the game, the Mutuals' pitcher gave an exhibition of throwing curve balls. This made such an impression on the boy that he vowed to teach himself this skill. It took a year of persistent effort, but at the age of fourteen, Amos Alonzo could crow to his mother, "I've got it! I can throw a curve ball!"

It was just one year later when he set his sights on a higher goal. He wrote, "My life really began on May 23, 1877, when I officially became a member of the First Presbyterian Church of Orange. I set aside my mischievous and careless youth and consecrated my life to the Christian ideals of virtue and service to others. I was inspired to mold my character on Christ's example and do good in His name." All of his life Amos Alonzo stayed true to his moral code and never gambled, smoked or drank alcohol, and he exercised regularly, so as to be pure and strong, in both mind and body, to best serve the Lord's purpose.

He was steadfast in his abstinence because as a young child he had witnessed the brutal miseries caused by drinking. He wrote, "The rendezvous in town of my playmates and myself was close by four saloons. Beer-drunken men were a daily sight and violent fights were common. We got our drama first-hand and in the raw from these saloons, and it was a continuing spectacle. Many of the children grew up under the shadow of drunkenness and the fear of the beatings that often followed. Good wages were squandered in these saloons and the children suffered grievously from the privations this caused. Many of my early playmates died well before their time was due."

In Sunday school, Amos Alonzo had learned about the great truths contained in the Bible and he began to see how his spiritual aspirations would be enhanced by furthering his education. By the end of his time at St. Mark's Grade School, he had such a desire for more knowledge that he asked his father for permission to attend Orange High School, which would require a tuition of sixty dollars a year, as it was outside their district. With his father's blessing, he earned the tuition himself by beating carpets, tending furnaces, spading gardens and working as a harvest hand on the salt meadows of New Jersey, although none of these jobs paid more than twenty-five cents an hour.

He attended high school for three years, each day running the mile from his home to school and back again, and for two years he pitched for his school's baseball team. He graduated in 1883 as one of only four students (two boys and two girls) to graduate that year. At high school, an idea began to form in his mind that grew to become his secret dream: He would go to Yale University and attend divinity school there to study for the ministry.

At that time, few students graduated from high school, much less college, and it was unthinkable that a poor farmer's son should have such an ambition. It was cause for hope, then, when he learned that his vice principal had worked his way through Yale and graduated in the class of 1878. Still, he did not reveal his dream to anyone until after his graduation.

When he finally told his father about his secret ambition, his father was encouraging, but he could not help him with financial support. Amos Alonzo then wrote to Yale about his admission and received in return a personal letter from Yale's president, Noah Porter, outlining the conditions of his acceptance. It was, therefore, a painful disappointment to him when he didn't pass the entrance exam and had to put his hopes for the future on hold.

It was his good fortune that he did not have to wait long, for at Christmas, George Gill, the other young man that he graduated with, came home for the holidays with stories about his life at Phillips Exeter Academy, a college preparatory school. George told him about some young men who were working their way through school there, and he urged Amos Alonzo to return with him to see if he could make his own way, too. Amos Alonzo was filled with enthusiasm and eager to go, but, for the first time, he saw his mother sick with fear and worry about his leaving home and he found that he could not calm her anxieties. Stagg later wrote, "She mourned as if she were going to lose me forever to the evil influences of drinking and gambling, and the other vices that wealthy young men could afford to

10

indulge themselves in." Yet, he held firm in his resolve to go. So despite his mother's tearful protests (and the embarrassment of having few clothes to take to school with him -- no overcoat, or even any underwear), he left for the train to Exeter wearing a borrowed suit from George Gill and only twenty-one dollars in his pocket earned from summer jobs.

The winter he spent at Phillips Exeter was cold and his life there rugged. He rented an unheated garret and budgeted a meager eighteen cents a day for food, purchasing soda crackers for five cents a pound and milk for three cents a quart. He resumed his habit of running and ran from garret to class to job, which kept him in shape and warm, as well. He studied Greek and Latin and also mathematics to prepare himself for Yale. However, it was his talent for playing baseball that attracted everyone's attention. He had his pitching skill, an aptitude for playing third base and a keen competitive drive. In midseason, the Exeter team chose him as their captain, which meant also being their "playing manager", with control over players both on and off the field. This gave him a good opportunity to build his leadership skills. He pitched the last three games of the season and performed so well that he began to make a name for himself in the biggest sport in college athletics at that time. That summer, he was offered a scholarship to Dartmouth if he would play baseball there. However, his desire to become a minister kept his goal set on divinity school, and in the fall of 1884, he fulfilled his dream, when he entered Yale's Halls of Ivy and he became an Eli.

PREPARING FOR A GREATER CALLING

At the start of his student days at Yale, Amos Alonzo continued the Spartan lifestyle he had begun at Exeter, as living at the university was even more expensive than the prep school. His reduced tuition of thirty dollars a semester (as a future divinity student) was still a financial hardship, so he rented another unheated attic room and confined himself to spending only five cents a day for breakfast and supper and ten cents a day for dinner. He soon learned that he could not sustain his strength on his near-starvation diet when he found himself on sick call for malnutrition. With a little help from his brothers and sisters (which he was no longer too proud to accept) and the money from several new jobs, he began to eat better and slowly regained his health. In order to toughen his body and strengthen his muscles, he created a training regimen for himself using the exercise apparatus in the university's gymnasium, which he performed daily for his entire career at Yale.

It was because of his studies and initially compromised health that he chose to participate in only one sport: Baseball. He found time for practice every day and, with an analytical approach, he relentlessly pursued his mastery of the game. He played for all of his six seasons at Yale, four as an undergraduate and two as a postgraduate and divinity student. Between the years 1886 and 1890, he pitched for five championship teams. In 52 appearances against Harvard and Princeton, Stagg won 42 times, lost on eight occasions and there were two ties. He pitched three one-hitters, struck out a total of 241 men and was never taken out of a game. The high point in his baseball career came in the spring of 1888, when he pitched a best-of-three series against Harvard to, in effect, determine the national championship. In the first game, he struck out sixteen men and allowed only two scratch hits, helping to shut out Harvard, 8-0. The next week, 12,000 people came to see the championship game. However, the previous triumph had taken its toll on Stagg. He later recalled, "I had snapped my arm so often in pitching 'drops' that I found I couldn't use an overhead windup at all, so I used an underhanded uprise instead. For three innings, I didn't allow one hit. I struck out 17 men, and we won the championship, 4-3.

"Being a pitcher is not merely throwing the ball. It is a battle of wits under high pressure. It is a desperate struggle in which the intensity of the heart's desire, supported by skill and cunning, determine the victory. How to get this as each batter is faced is something that each pitcher himself must determine. I stimulated my will to win during the progress of games by frequently praying, 'Help me to do my best.' And in more than one game, I prayed that prayer before every ball I pitched. We won most of our games, but when we lost, my conscience was clear that I had done my best for Yale."

"Jumping Jack" Jones, a professional pitcher who was covering that game for the *New Haven Register*, wrote. "While nearly all pitchers are limited to one style of delivery, Stagg could throw curves from a straight-arm or elbow-bent style, and he had a supplementary wrist motion to call upon, as well. He always has something new to throw in a pinch."

In 1887, Yale played an exhibition game with the professional players of Boston's National League team. The Boston Braves (now known as the Atlanta Braves) were led by the famous Michael "King" Kelly, who as the major leagues' highest-paid player, earned what was then the whopping sum of $4,000 a season (when $1000 a year could provide a middle class lifestyle). He had batted .388 the previous year and had scored a remarkable 155 runs, but he was also the inventor of the dangerous "hook slide" -- a slide into base with cleats up and targeted at a vulnerable area, intended to injure and perhaps maim an opposing player. He was an intimidating adversary, but he met his nemesis in Stagg. "Double A" Amos Alonzo struck out the "King" in the ninth inning, needing only three pitches to do it.

This stunning performance earned Stagg proposals from seven of the eight National League clubs. The Pittsburgh Pirates made him an offer that beat even the "King's" deal -- $5,000 a season! The New York Giants wanted to pay Stagg $3,000 for only three months of pitching (and he wouldn't have to spend a day at training camp), but Stagg turned away every offer. He had begun to see that baseball, as played by the "professionals", had become a disreputable game. It was being played in a mean-spirited atmosphere of bullying and foul language and there was widespread gambling. It even was known that some major leaguers used cocaine (There were no federal laws against narcotics back then.). Stagg had decided long ago that his goals could not be found in this direction and absolutely no amount of money could induce him to take part in this type of "sporting" life. As he put it, "There are saloons in big league ballparks."

It was in his senior year at Yale, 1888, that Amos Alonzo started to play the game that was to give him even greater success than baseball and help him create his sports legacy. He hadn't played football before then for fear of injuring his pitching arm, yet he was drawn to the rough and tumble of a sport that was played with the same exuberance and cheerful camaraderie of the games of his youth. Football wasn't so much a contest of individual skill as was baseball, but a game where teamwork counted most, and he enjoyed its spirit of good fellowship. Best of all for him, football was a running game! It turned out that his daily runs and exercise routines, plus his other healthful habits, were the perfect training for a football player. They had built his five-foot, six-inch frame into 157 pounds of powerful muscle and given him stamina to spare. It seemed that from the time he first set foot on Yale's campus, he was destined for the game of football.

MR. STAGG BEGINS A LIFE IN THE PIGSKIN GAME

In the 1880's, American football was still in its infancy, having begun in 1869 as a form of the English game of rugby. It was, like rugby, a "gentleman's game", played mostly by the sons of the east coast's social elite, and, at that, only on the fields of four Ivy League schools -- Harvard, Princeton, Columbia, Yale -- and Rutgers. The sport had been "fathered" by Walter Camp, who had played on Yale's teams from 1876 to 1881. Camp was never actually a fulltime coach, though, because of the demands of his position as executive of a watch company. However, his strong ethical basis combined with a zeal for the sport enabled him to make this new American game something apart from rugby and soccer. He envisioned a tough, physical sport containing elements of strategy and skill that would always be open to new ideas to make the game better. Camp invented a rule that truly revolutionized football and completely separated it from rugby and soccer: A team must advance a certain number of yards, or else give up the ball. This idea of Camp's resulted in a pause in action between each play to allow the ball to be spotted and the yardage kept track of. The pause in action also allowed for intensive strategizing. For nearly fifty years, Walter Camp was renowned for his part in the development of football rules and he treated this role as a sacred trust literally up to the very moment of his death (He died suddenly during the recess of a rules committee meeting.). Later, he and publisher Casper Whitney helped bring new prominence to the game with their concept of choosing an "All-American" team, and they selected their very first one in 1889.

Camp was also a mentor to Yale's football team captains. It was the custom for the captains to gather at Camp's home in the evenings and discuss the day's happenings at practice, listen to his suggestions for improving the team's execution and plan strategy for upcoming games. Long before women's lib appeared on the horizon, he received tremendous help from his wife, Alice. A true student of the game herself, "Allie" Camp walked the sidelines during practices and took lengthy notes. In the evening, she would not only review her notes with Walter, but would also sit in on the strategy sessions in which forthcoming games were discussed. As a result of all of this, those involved with leading Yale's teams not only instilled the important principles of football, but were able to do it in a wholesome atmosphere and be in a position to invoke rigid training rules and demand that Yale football players acquire good habits.

While Walter Camp provided the environment in which the new game of football flourished, it was William "Pa" Corbin who introduced Amos Alonzo Stagg to the sport. Corbin was a tall, rawboned New Englander with a long, lean face and handlebar moustache that gave him a majestic air. He also rowed crew for the "Elis", which strengthened his octopus-like arms, so that nothing got by him on the football field. He was a commanding figure in his playing gear, which included a white turtle necked jersey with a big blue "Y" sewn on and a baseball cap perched on his head. The handlebar moustache made him look older than his years, and together with his leadership qualities and knowledge of football, led to his being nicknamed "Pa".

Pa Corbin took his role of team captain seriously. "The captain should be the real leader," said Corbin. "He should be able to say, 'Come on,' instead of 'Go on.' He should be a strategist, always checking the signals and often changing them. Quarterbacks may come and go, but the captain should always be largely responsible for the tactics and the success of the plays." Corbin demanded unconditional loyalty from anyone wishing to play for Yale, was strict, but fair and laid down the law to his teammates; a law grounded upon principles of moral conduct. He never cursed or used profanity. Corbin's persona attracted A.A. Stagg, a 27-year-old divinity student, and also drew in Pudge Heffelfinger, a millionaire's son from Minnesota who came off as a "Paul Bunyan with a 'Y' on his chest". (Pudge Heffelfinger became the first professional football player when he was paid $500 in 1892 to play a game for the Allegheny (Pennsylvania) Athletic Association. In 1916, at the age of 49, he scrimmaged against the Yale varsity to help them prepare for Harvard. In 1920, at the age of 53, he played 50 minutes for the East All-Stars against the Ohio All-Stars in Columbus, Ohio. His last gridiron appearance was in 1930, at the age of 63, in an all-star game in Minneapolis, Minnesota. Heffelfinger lived to be 86.)

While reminiscing about Corbin, Heffelfinger stated, "The worst he ever hollered if he got mad was, 'You big cow!' Corbin was a rangy, hard-fighting center who could take all kinds of punishment and a man who had a head and used it on the football field. He was the captain of the first team I ever played on and I owe much of what I learned

18

about the game to this great player, and the inspiration he provided."

Football historian Bruce Stewart wrote of Pa Corbin's discovering Heffelfinger when, "Pudge was playing in a freshman scrimmage stacked with fifteen men per side. Corbin watched in amazement as Pudge nabbed a low punt and ran over everyone except the last, unfortunate tackler, who tackled him at the expense of a broken hip.

"Corbin was a hard man to get a compliment out of, though, so all he said to Heffelfinger was, 'Hey you, freshman! That was a nice run. Ever play the line?'

"'No sir,' stammered Heffelfinger.

"'Come over to the varsity field with me,' ordered Corbin, 'and see what you can do at guard. We need more linemen than backs.

"'Have you got a nickname?'

"'No,' answered Pudge, remembering how his dad warned him not to use his high school nickname 'Pudge' at Yale.

"'Fine, we'll call you 'Heff'. Your real name is too long,' announced Corbin."

"In spite of being triple-teamed that day, his shins and nose smashed," added Bruce Stewart, "Heff impressed the varsity enough to make first team guard. But as the season wore on, his teammates worried that he was too nice to opposing players. 'Heff, you remind me of a big cow,' Pa Corbin growled. 'You're too good-natured. Rattle their teeth on every tackle after this or turn in your jersey! Friendship ceases when the whistle blows.'"

The type of gridiron game Stagg played was almost completely different from today's football. All that has stayed the same are the goal posts and the width of the field. Eleven men played on a side, each man planned on playing the entire game, substitutions were held to a minimum and there were hardly any time outs. So, more than anything else, each contest was a test of endurance, yet as close to being a pure form of play that football would ever be.

"I started to learn to play football at Yale in 1884, only four years after the teams had consisted of fifteen players on a side (the same as rugby)," recalled Mr. Stagg. "That was when touchdowns counted two points, kicking a goal after touchdown two points, a safety one point and a field goal five points. Before I finished playing, the touchdown and safety had each doubled in value.

"In 1884, tackling was limited to the waist and above. It was lowered to above the knees in 1888. Line-blocking was legal, but blocking as we now know it was unknown and illegal in 1884.

"In the early eighties, the linemen on offense stood erect with spread feet, extended arms and closed hands; while the linemen on the defense stood opposite and sparred with their opponents -- literally tried to punch them in the face -- in an effort to break down their barriers and get at the runner." Stagg's description of football's earliest days made the sport appear to be the equivalent of seven MMA or boxing matches being fought on each snap of the ball.

"A single referee did the officiating from 1884 until 1887, when the umpire was added," continued Stagg. "It was the heyday for a good boxer and slugger type of player, for there was no penalty for unnecessary roughness. In my time, I can think of two or three men who were notorious for their rough play.

20

"Up to 1888, the backs were playing loosely, well back and spread, ready to receive a pitchout from the quarterback in order to run with the ball or punt it. They had to depend largely on their native ability to gain ground through fleetness, dodging and cleverness in straight-arming and breaking tackles; since there was no organized method of blocking as a team.

"There were no hired coaches in my playing days. We learned our football, as well as the rules, through daily scrimmage and through the older players and from their advice; and, of course, the spasmodic coaching of local and visiting alumni who returned for a few days' visit to the campus before the big games with Harvard and Princeton. The strategy of play was handed down through the captain and such seniors as had the privilege of discussing football tactics and strategies with the great master of early Yale football -- Walter Camp.

"The signals were words, phrases and sentences which seemed to be used for stimulating the play of the team -- such as, 'Play hard.' 'Don't let down.' Keep fighting.' etc. -- but were actually code words for our play. In our championship year of 1888, the word signals meant nothing and captain 'Pa' Corbin actually gave hand signals from his position at center as he stood with his right foot on the ball, poised to snap it back with his foot to our quarterback. His hand signals were a form of 'sign language' given by placing his hand or hands on some particular part of his body to indicate the play. He played wearing his baseball cap and the different ways he positioned his baseball cap were even part of the signal system.

"The quarterback handled the ball on nearly every play. The center's job of snapping the ball back with his foot, so that the quarterback could catch it on the rebound and pitch it quickly to the runner was high art and required much practice to prevent fumbling. I recall that the centers and quarterbacks practiced their skills in the gym nearly every morning during a free period.

"Throughout the time I played, the game was supposed to start with a kickoff, but the subterfuge was conceived of 'inch-kicking', in which there was the pretense of a kick. The ball went a few inches, then was picked up by the kicking team's center. The kicking team then formed a wedge, the center would hand the ball back to another player inside the wedge and the slow-moving mass of players clinging to one another would move forward in a slow lockstep run. The strategy was to open an aperture at a certain point of the wedge through which the imprisoned runner would dart for his escape and gain yardage for his team.

"Profound changes took place during the period that I played which revolutionized the game. The rules of 1888 did away with the use of widely extended arms of the linemen on offense, which led to holding their opponents. Lowering the arms naturally constricted the lines, because the linemen were now forced to actually block their opponents. The halfbacks also came in closer in order to be able to provide additional blocking for the runner. The linemen started to play lower and develop their individual techniques. In my final year of play, 1889, our center, Bert Hanson, bent over and bounced the ball back between his legs with his hand, which was the first time that had ever been done. The fullback and the halves that year stood quite close in, in what basically came to be known as the T-Formation.

"Changing from having linemen in a set, fixed position during the 1884-1887 period to one affording more freedom of movement very quickly gave an impetus to individual initiative. George Woodruff, then a Yale guard, found that he could be of advantage to the runner by moving around on the attack to the other side of the center, and the famous Heffelfinger expanded the idea by swinging out in either direction as the accompanying bodyguard for Yale's halfbacks. Walter Camp once said of Pudge Heffelfinger, 'Pudge was the fastest big man I ever saw.' On defense, he not only could cover his own position, but a good part of the space on the other side of the line as well. He was also the most effective in leading interference around end.'"

"While playing at left end in 1888 and at right end in 1889," continued Mr. Stagg, "I began to realize my freedom for maneuvering when my team was on the offensive and in the latter year I found that by anticipating and lining up a couple of feet behind the scrimmage line, I could precede the fullback on his plunges to the opposite side of the center, as well as swing around ahead of the halfback and cut him off."

"Freshmen were eligible for the varsity then," recalled Pudge Heffelfinger. "Moreover, the Yale captain outranked the coach and could pick his own team and decide what plays to use. The coach, in this case Walter Camp, was really just an adviser."

"Our workouts stressed live tackling, man against man in the open field," continued Heffelfinger. "In 1888, we scrimmaged for one solid hour every afternoon, except on Wednesday and Saturday when we played games with outside teams. I used to lose four or five pounds in these scrimmages. Game days seemed like a vacation to us.

On Sunday, our 'day of rest', we took six-mile hikes across country!

"Throughout my college career, we had about 500 students watching practice every afternoon. We felt that the student body was behind us, and the students felt that they were part of the team. If you had missed a tackle or a block during practice, they yelled at you and called you a bum when they met you after the workout. They kept us on our toes with their criticism, because it hurt our pride to hear the campus talking about our mistakes.

"I was the heaviest man on the team at 190 pounds, but, we were strong, durable, hard as nails and fast. Nothing lumbering or ponderous about that bunch. George Woodruff and I flanked Pa Corbin in the middle of the line. Woodruff was a picturesque character. He wore a coonskin cap and sported a set of whiskers when he first came to Yale from a Pennsylvania Dutch homestead. Life on the farm had so developed his muscles that he broke all strength test records at Yale.

"Alonzo Stagg was better known as a pitcher than as an end. He was 5' 6" tall and weighed a mere 157 pounds when he played on Corbin's team. For all his Biblical precepts, Stagg had a way of pulling foxy tricks. He always thought two plays ahead of the other fellow. After the college season was over each fall, he organized a barnstorming team called the Christian Workers of Springfield, Massachusetts. One of his pet trick plays -- the 'Dead Man Hoax' -- smacked of chicanery. When the ball was snapped, Stagg's whole team ran toward the left flank as though for an end run, except the chap who took the snap. This fellow flopped down on his belly with the ball concealed beneath him, and literally played dead. This was back in the days when a play wasn't over until the ball carrier was not only tackled, but actually pinned to the

24

ground, so when the opponents rushed over to stop the fake sweep, the 'corpse' would leap to his feet and run like hell. They made a lot of touchdowns with this rather unchristian like play.

"I still have an old woodcut illustration of Stagg administering a 'ministerial uppercut' to an opponent in the heat of a game."

"Pudge Heffelfinger was remembered most for his method of breaking up the 'Flying Wedge'," recalled Stagg. "He did this by leaping into the air, crashing through the wedge and landing on the runner inside who had the ball. The usual method of meeting the wedge had been to dive under it and try to trip the players, or just try to crash straight through." Heffelfinger first used his new method in the Yale-Princeton game of 1888, which in those days was regarded as a contest for the national championship.

Heffelfinger stated when he recalled that classic game, "The 1888 match was played at the old Polo Grounds in New York City, and the Fifth Avenue Hotel on 23rd Street was the Yale headquarters. On game day the lobby was always filled with hero worshipers. The team rode a tallyho draped with Yale blue bunting from the hotel along Fifth Avenue, then through Central Park to the football grounds. We all sat on top of the carriage and waved at the pretty girls who flirted with us, or jeered at the Princeton rooters giving us the Bronx Cheer.

"That ride was not without incident, however. The horses got away from our driver, and we hit a hansom cab in Central Park. 'Hey, youse guys!' bellowed that cabbie, 'ain't you got enough trouble with Princeton today without lookin' for more?'

"While riding up Fifth Avenue, Pa Corbin warned us about Princeton's 'V-Wedge'. Pa looked plenty worried. That Princeton Tiger wedge was a terrible thing to face. It simply murdered the men up front. The man at the apex of the V put the ball in play and the runner was screened by the phalanx. We met the lead man by socking him in the jaw with our hands, but they rolled over us just the same. Then I got an idea. Why not fight fire with fire and crash the wedge head-on in midair? They'd throw you off the field for brutality if you tried anything like that today, but nobody penalized me, though Princeton, of course, protested vigorously. As the wedge formed, I backed away to get a running start, put on full steam ahead, took off like a broad jumper, knees doubled up, and crashed full tilt against the chest of the chap leading the V. The impact of my 190 pounds shooting through the air like a projectile caused the wedge to shiver and collapse.

"Princeton's Hector Cowan was furious. 'Hey, you big moose, you're going to kill somebody!' he yelled at me. Cowan was a chunky, deep-chested fellow, built like a smokehouse. He had the strongest shoulders and arms I've ever been up against, and his stubby legs drove like pistons when he carried the ball. He could carry a couple of tacklers on his back, yet he was plenty fast in the open. 'I'll quit it if you stop using that V-Wedge!' I shouted back at Hector. Naturally, they wouldn't make that deal. They foxed me the next time I tried it by ducking low and warding off my dive with upflung arms. Luck was with me, though, on one critical play when I spotted a gap in the V and went through to nail their ball carrier Snake Ames for a big loss. That spoiled a Princeton scoring opportunity."

"Our opponents soon took up Heffelfinger's method," added Stagg, "so I suggested having two

26

'out-runners' (I was one of them) go ahead of the wedge and block off the center and the guard on the side that we wished our runner to emerge from. This was my first actual contribution to football strategy. As to my personal contribution in that game, I tackled the famous Knowlton 'Snake' Ames again and again and he didn't make any yardage around my end."

"Neither team made a touchdown, as those tough lines played each other to a standstill," continued Heffelfinger. "We finally won, though, 10 to 0, on Billy Bull's dropkicks. I can still see him now booting the first field goal with blood streaming down his face from a head cut. We wore no helmets then, and just soft-quilted pads on our shoulders and elbows. Field goals counted for five points. Bull's second field goal was kicked from a sharp angle on the 37-yard line with barely a minute to play. He stood like a blood-spattered statue while the Tigers put on one hellacious rush. But he kept his head down and his eyes rooted on the ball. The kick was perfect."

"We were unbeaten (13-0) and won the championship that year," added Stagg, "and outscored our opponents 694 to 0."

Stagg first earned his college expenses by waiting on tables in the university's dining halls, but during his senior year, he was paid an annual salary of $425 (when $400 per year was the equivalent of an entry level salary) to be a sports editor of *The Yale News*. In August 1889, after Stagg was paid $80 to author "Baseball for Amateurs" (published by Harper and Bros. of New York), Walter Camp offered him even more money for writing articles on football to appear in publications Camp was connected with. Amos Alonzo wrote Camp and politely turned him down, stating, "I have already learned from my five years at Yale that I cannot do many different things well at the same time, and there would be a resulting tumble -- e.g., when study and athletics meet, study gets fooled every time.

"I have been having a fine time here at Yale this summer studying Hebrew six hours every day for the past five weeks. Even with my being engrossed heart and soul in Hebrew, the Yale football captain Charlie Gill had the presumption to speak to me about playing football next fall."

During the following season, a story appeared in the local papers about Stagg's new invention of a tackling dummy. "He has rolled up a mattress to about the size of a man's body and suspended it in the gymnasium," the article read. "Mattresses are laid on the floor under this and now the men can run half the length of the building and tackle the suspended mattress to their hearts' content, never fearing a fall on the floor because the mattresses will protect them."

"In 1889, I was changed over from right end to left end," recalled Mr. Stagg. "We were a good team and lost only one game, but it was to Princeton, and, as a result, Princeton won the championship that year." It was the first losing football game Amos Alonzo Stagg had ever played in.

"During that Princeton game," continued Stagg, "Josh Hartwell, Yale's right end, had a knee injury and was badly crippled. Snake Ames, their very fine fullback, ran around his end several times. Three times, though, I crossed over behind our own line and tackled him when he reversed his field and appeared on his way to a touchdown." This had not been tried before on any football field. Stagg's innovative defensive concept is now known as "pursuit".

"I'm sure that performance had a lot to do with my being selected to the very first All-American team, along with Ames, which was chosen after that season," added Stagg.

With all his achievements in football, Amos Alonzo's top priority was still becoming a minister, and an inspiring sermon he heard at Yale kept him focused on his goal. "The theme was based on Horace Mann's words to the graduating class at Oberlin: 'Be ashamed to die until you have done something for your fellow men,'" recalled Mr. Stagg. "This is what I tried to pattern my life after."

After earning his Bachelor of Arts degree, Stagg was certain that he was bound for a lifetime in the pulpit spreading the word of the Lord. He returned to Yale for additional courses before divinity school and became student secretary of the local YMCA. Many years later, *Guideposts Magazine's* Van Varner described the events which changed the course of the Grand Old Man's life when he wrote, "Each Wednesday night, there was a YMCA meeting and frequently Stagg ventured forth to other towns and cities on deputations. It was not unusual for Stagg to speak at these meetings, but it was very unusual if he spoke well. Once on his feet, his mind grew fuzzy. He stumbled over words, groped for phrases that would not come, left in obscurity the points that he most wanted to make clear. Throughout the following school year, he plugged away at Hebrew and philosophy -- and fought to acquire the ability to speak. Though he had no trouble expressing himself when counseling or in small groups, a formal talk seemed beyond his powers.

"Again and again he practiced speaking alone, only to fail in public. He prayed; still there was no noticeable improvement. 'How can I be a minister,' he agonized. 'How can I spread the word of God if I cannot speak?'

"By the time that summer was over, his anguish had heightened. He feared the failure that faced him and he looked back upon all those years of work, sacrifice and preparation for this one objective with a sickening feeling of waste.

"And then slowly, imperceptibly at first, he came to realize that it was not necessary to wear the cloth to represent his religion effectively. Every man, he reasoned, can, and should, do what he is best qualified to do, but in such a way that his principles shine for all to see. Ministers are ambassadors of Christ; so can all men in all professions be.

"'What are my own special talents?' Stagg asked himself.

"The answer came quickly: Athletics. If he could win athletes to Christ doing the job he had hoped to do as a minister, would he not really be reaching the same goal?"

Years later, Rev. Myron Herrell, Stagg's pastor at Stockton's Central Methodist Church, noted, "Play, for him, was not an escape from life any more, but a goal of life. He made clear his view that sports may constitute preparation for life; on the field the man may develop the attitude and spirit which make him ready to live. He became an eloquent exponent of the philosophy of playing for the fun of the game.

"St. Paul referred to a 'prize'. Everybody competes in athletics, Paul said, but only one gets the prize. The ultimate score in living, however, the prize worth the power drive down the field of life, is not an exclusive award. It is shared, if, in the process, you have helped someone else to find a better life."

It may seem surprising that an aspiring minister would choose such a drastic change in purpose and begin coaching such a rough sport as football, especially Amos Alonzo Stagg, who was a remarkably talented *baseball* player. Competing at the highest level of baseball, however, meant playing professionally, and, in the late nineteenth century, the lifestyle of many major leaguers encompassed the use of alcohol and tobacco. Gambling was also a part of the atmosphere. Football, on the other hand was essentially a collegiate sport then and Stagg viewed it as something that could be developed into an excellent means of instilling good, moral habits.

With his new career goal, Mr. Stagg entered the new International YMCA College (now Springfield College) in 1890 to study physical education. While there, he asked and was given permission to organize football and baseball teams for that school. A few weeks later, he received a telegram from Dr. William Rainey Harper inviting him to a breakfast meeting in New York's sumptuous Murray Hill Hotel. A new university was to be founded in Chicago -- the University of Chicago -- endowed by the great oil wealth of John D. Rockefeller. Harper had been selected to be the university's first president.

There had been a Baptist college of the same name in Chicago, but it had closed due to financial problems in

1886. With Rockefeller backing, however, Harper had hopes of heading the greatest university in the nation with a faculty and administration constantly striving to be the best in the world. He planned on bringing this magnificent dream into reality by establishing a great liberal educational institution that would have all branches of education combined to serve the needs of all types of students; a radical departure from the first colleges in America, most of which originated as schools of theology. Harper's vision included having a full-time athletic director with faculty standing; for he believed that physical education and sports were an integral part of a well-rounded education. At first, some U of C administrators and faculty members were concerned that competitive sports would keep students from their studies, but President Harper disagreed, maintaining that, "The athletic field is one of the university's laboratories and by no means the least important one."

Harper's thoughts naturally first turned to Yale, his alma mater, as he began assembling the school's first faculty. Of all Yale men, Amos Alonzo Stagg, to whom he had taught a course in biblical history, was Harper's first choice for the new role of athletic director. "I first became acquainted with Mr. Stagg when he was at the height of his student athletic career at Yale," William Rainey Harper later recalled. "For three years, he was a student in my classes. An attachment was formed between us which grew closer every year."

While they breakfasted at the fancy Murray Hill Hotel, President Harper said to the young coach of simple tastes, "I'll give you $1500 a year if you come to Chicago."

Stagg was silent.

"I'll give you $2000."

Stagg continued to maintain a thoughtful silence.

"...and an assistant professorship," added Harper.

Harper realized that, though Stagg may have had simple tastes, he wasn't easy to please. The university president wasn't easily dissuaded, though, and finally said, "Well, all right, I'll give you $2500 and an associate professorship."

There was a long pause before Stagg finally replied, "I'll come if you let me combine athletics and physical education in one department."

Years later, Stagg explained, "I kept thinking it over. I suppose Dr. Harper thought it was money. It wasn't at all. Money never was an object with me. I had studied for the ministry and believed I could perform as great a service in athletics as I could in the pulpit. While Dr. Harper was talking during that breakfast, I was wondering if Chicago would be a better 'field to till' than the east."

"It was evident," Harper later stated, "that Stagg had certain ideals about athletic work and of athletic policy, and he made it clear that his coming to Chicago was dependent wholly upon his having every opportunity to work out these ideals. He came; he was given the opportunity he desired and, as a result, it is not too much to say that 'western' athletics were altogether transformed."

His salary of $2500 per year made Stagg the highest paid man in football at that point in time. Most early coaches worked strictly at their alma maters as unpaid volunteers. The usual practice was to have the previous team captain or another graduated player train the team and the wages of any coaches who were actually paid couldn't compare with Stagg's salary.

After another meeting with President Harper in January 1891, Stagg wrote to his sister Pauline. "I had one very pleasant surprise during our conversation. I had been in doubt of what Dr. Harper's attitude toward athletics would be. I feared that, in his race for intellectual achievements, he might disregard intercollegiate athletics and be content with just enough exercise to keep the body in fair condition for mental work. But in answer to my question of what his attitude was about intercollegiate athletics, he said, 'I am most heartily in favor of them. I want you to develop teams which we can send around the country and knock out all the colleges. If you do that, I'll give them a palace car and a vacation.'

"These words made me very happy. I am so very fond of outdoor sports; but more than this, it will be sure to create a strong college spirit, which means so much to a college boy's life. And last and best of all, it will give me such a fine chance to do Christian work among the boys who are sure to have the most influence. Win the athletes of any college for Christ and you have the strongest working element attainable in college life. Oh, I am so happy and thankful for the outlook!"

The University of Chicago wouldn't open its doors until October 1892, and Stagg didn't waste the intervening time. The next two years were the beginning of his coaching career -- at Springfield College in Springfield, Massachusetts. There were only 47 men in the student body then, but Stagg quickly developed football teams, nicknamed the "Stubby Christians", which fared creditably among New England colleges.

"Jim Naismith was on that team and I selected him to be the center; even though he weighed only 154 pounds and I had a 195-pound man at one of the end positions," recalled Stagg. "When he asked why, I replied that, 'You seem to do the most diabolical things in the most gentlemanly manner.' Naismith thought about it, then told me I was absolutely right. Jim never failed to give tit for tat, and always with a smile on his face.

"We were playing the Boston Athletic Club in 1891, and in the early part of the game they stopped our running attack over the middle, which had been so effective in all of our previous games. Jim was playing center, of course, and I called him over to the sidelines and quietly asked him what was the matter. Jim told me the trouble was due to the fact the Athletic Club's center was playing right in front of him, with another player positioned as a linebacker right behind the center. The instant Jim would snap the ball, the linebacker would literally push the center into Naismith. 'I've always been able to make a hole against any center I've met,' said Jim, 'but I'm not able to make a hole against a catapulted center. But you leave it to me and I'll fix him next time.'

"So on the very next play, Jim snapped the ball, but the instant he did it, he stepped sideways out of the path of the catapulted center; who landed flat on his face on gravelly ground and got his face badly skinned in the bargain. Immediately afterwards, Jim overheard the Athletic Club center tell the player who was pushing him not to do it anymore. From that moment on, our plays began to work havoc and we beat them by a large score."

"That same year at Springfield College," continued Stagg, "I arranged for the first-ever indoor football game; played in New York's Madison Square Garden on December 12, 1890. We played a team called the 'Yale Consolidated Team', which had five former Yale varsity players, including Pudge Heffelfinger and they won from us, 16-10."

Stagg coached two seasons at Springfield College; then the University of Chicago opened its doors and it was time to move on.

"At the opening of the University of Chicago in 1892," said Stagg, "I was made an associate professor and Director of the Department of Physical Culture and Athletics, as well as a regular member of the faculty. This was the first time a football coach was ever given such responsibility.

"I became the pioneer athletic director. Hitherto, in all colleges and universities, athletics had been under the control of a student athletic association. Following my ideas, the University of Chicago was the first to place athletics, all physical activities, all athletic properties and equipment under the control of my department. This department, without the assistance of students, arranged programs for all physical activities, arranged intercollegiate games and was responsible for the sale of tickets and for receipts. An athletic fund was created, with the gate receipts placed in the hands of the university comptroller; but to be disbursed on my OK. This became the prototype for what has been used by most universities and colleges."

In the case of the University of Chicago, though, absolutely none of the money in the athletic fund was to come from university funds.

When the young professor arrived at his new place of employment, he found that it was located on the south side of Chicago amid a considerable area of prairie land lying to the south of Hyde Park and to the north of Woodlawn -- two of the city's finest residential neighborhoods. Plans were underway to hold a world's fair -- the Columbian Exposition -- in nearby Jackson Park. The fair's organizers bought a strip of ground to be used as a "Midway Plaisance" to connect Jackson Park, at the east end of the fair, with Washington Park, which constituted the western edge of the fair. The new buildings of the University of Chicago were erected north of this area and, over the course of time, the entire campus became known as "The Midway".

In 1892, however, The Midway was still a cow pasture. Paved streets were miles away from the new university. Most of the university's money came from John D. Rockefeller, who was not very popular with the public or the press. Another complication was that, even though he had graduated from Yale and had done postgraduate work, Stagg was not welcomed with open arms by all members of the faculty as a fellow intellectual. He was confronted by individuals in the academic community who considered him an overpaid, over-muscled rustic seeking to spread a specious dogma of "muscular Christianity". For a long time "big and dumb" was considered by some as synonymous with "football". Unfortunately, this stereotype has persisted, but things began to change; thanks to surveys by such publications as

Forbes Magazine which revealed that more than 90 percent of CEOs and members of boards of directors had some experience in intercollegiate athletics. Stagg, however, didn't have the support of any such surveys when he started his career at the U of C.

When classes first began on October 1, 1892, only 14 players went out for Chicago's first football team. Most of them had absolutely no experience in the sport, and Stagg himself was forced to not only play, but also serve as Chicago's first team captain -- at 30 years of age. One of the experienced players was Andy Wyant, who had played four years at Bucknell. Wyant had transferred because, as he later stated, "After Bucknell had defeated Cornell in 1891, Dr. Harper contacted me and invited me to enroll at Chicago." If a similar situation were to occur today, the story of a university president recruiting a football player from another college would dominate ESPN for weeks.

"The dawn of athletics at the University of Chicago did not break effulgently, although, like the university itself, it was noisily trumpeted," recalled Stagg. "I had agreed to come to a new university two years before there was a building completed. There were fewer than 500 students when it opened. All during my directorship, there was no appropriation of money for athletics. They were expected to pay for themselves.

"During the initial football season of 1892, we deferred payment on as much of our simple equipment as possible and I advanced from my own pocket the money for things we could not get on deferred payment. Our equipment was very modest. For our squad of fourteen players, the cost of the equipment was less than what was paid fifty years later for a single player in a big university.

We wore canvas and not silk pants in those days; and thigh, hip and shoulder pads had not yet appeared on the horizon. The seven intercollegiate games scheduled for the season of 1892 were all arranged after the opening of the university on October 1st, which was two or three weeks after the other institutions had started their practices." The hurriedly arranged slate even forced the U of C to play four November games in only twelve days.

Even before the university held its first class, the Board of Trustees had arbitrarily selected a goldenrod shade of yellow as the school color. It did not take long for Mr. Stagg to realize a change was necessary since, "The yellow ran, soiled easily and had a regrettable symbolism which our opponents were not above commenting on." It took two years for Stagg to have the team color changed to maroon and the nickname "Maroons" adopted.

Chicago's very first game was a practice contest against Hyde Park High School, and Stagg's team won, 12 to 0. Five more practice games were played and won before Chicago had its baptism into intercollegiate competition.

The Maroons' first-ever college opponent was Northwestern University from the Chicago suburb of Evanston. Northwestern's nickname then was "The Fighting Methodists" and they had an eight-year edge in experience, having played football since 1884. With Stagg and Wyant playing, Chicago gained a 0-0 tie. The game was played in the old White Sox Park and the Maroons' share of the gate receipts was $22.65. A week later, though, Northwestern exacted revenge.

"We were beaten in that contest with Northwestern University, 6 to 4," remembered Stagg, "and we had to stand, in addition to the defeat, the absolute knowledge that we were a better team and played better than they. We outplayed them on all sides, keeping the ball in their territory most of the time. And yet, they won the game. The touchdown which they made and from which they kicked a goal was the result of a ruse in which the ball was not fairly put in play. But aside from the rules-bending, they were able to score a touchdown as a result of one man, our quarterback, disobeying the injunctions I had repeatedly made to him that year.

"The 'N Boys' formed a 'Flying Wedge' and our end men should have kept out of the mass and watch for the very thing Northwestern did: Instead of pushing straight ahead in a mass, they faked doing so, then ran out from behind it. We had our quarterback playing 20 yards back of the line, but he missed tackling the ball carrier and the ball carrier made the touchdown. This was done in the last minute of the first half.

"We had the ball in the start of play of the second half. Using our version of the Flying Wedge, we made a gain of 20 yards on one play, then continued to gain steadily without once losing it until we carried the ball across the goal line. The touchdown was made along one of the far corners of the end zone, which resulted in a very difficult angle for me to kick the extra point. The ball was also slippery from the wet grounds. My kick failed.

"We nearly scored again, but could not quite do so before the darkness made it necessary to call the game. It was a hard experience, because, with good umpiring and refereeing, we could've beaten them ten times out of ten. I worked very hard to win a victory, doing nearly all of the running and always making good gains. I wasn't a whit discouraged, though. We did very well for a small institution, and a new one at that. I had only a small number to pick from, for the undergraduates were the only men interested in football. Looking back on it, a defeat was the best thing for us at that point." Stagg definitely had his players' attention after that loss and they made sure to follow his "injunctions" from then on.

Later that season, Chicago traveled out of town for the first time to play a game, but they had to pose as Lehigh University to do so. Lehigh was scheduled to play the University of Michigan at Toledo, Ohio on November 12th and the contest had been heavily advertised. Shortly before the game, however, the Lehigh coach sent word that his team wouldn't be able to make it. Michigan appealed to Stagg for help and he and his squad caught a train at the last minute to get to Toledo in time. Michigan won, 18 to 10, and the crowd never found out that Lehigh wasn't on the field.

Chicago's only victory that trail-breaking year was over Illinois, 10 to 4, on Thanksgiving Day. The first half of that game ended in a 4-4 tie and the contest remained tied until darkness began to fall and time was running out, then Stagg took matters into his own hands. He dashed around left end to score a touchdown, which counted for four points back then, and added another two points by kicking a "goal after touchdown". The Illini, however, later won a return game. Shortly before that second game with Illinois, Stagg suffered an injury during practice and was unable to play. But at the invitation of the Illini, he refereed the game -- an early tribute to his reputation of integrity. According to Paul Stagg, "My father's reputation for forthright honesty and sense of fair play preceded him to the midwest. It resulted from an incident during his years of coaching at Springfield College, when he went out onto the field and objected to a penalty called upon an opponent."

Before the university's opening, President Harper had asked Stagg if he thought he could work with the large number of "girl students" expected to enroll. "I told him I thought I could," recalled Mr. Stagg. "He then said, 'I don't believe you'll be able to do it all alone. You'll have to get married and let a 'Mrs. Stagg' help you.'" Little did anyone realize how prophetic that statement would be.

Among the first group of women students at the University of Chicago was Stella Robertson from upstate New York. Dr. Marc Jantzen, dean of the University of the Pacific's School of Education and the Staggs' neighbor in Stockton, recalled that, "Stella enrolled as a freshman in the fall of 1892. She came from Albion, New York, a small town about 20 miles from Buffalo. Stella had graduated from Albion High School at the age of fourteen, then passed New York regents examinations -- which included tests in Greek and Latin -- in order to enter the brand new university. In addition to being very bright, her forebears were among the earliest settlers of this nation and could be traced all the way back to the Mayflower. Some of them fought the British in the American Revolution."

"As she later told it," continued Dr. Jantzen, "Stella could not afford to go home for Christmas that first year. So, she and several other women who were also staying in the dormitory during the holidays decided to find out more about the new sport of football which was being played at the university. At Stella's suggestion, they invited the coach, Amos Alonzo Stagg, to speak to them.

"From that contact developed a relationship between Stella Robertson and Amos Alonzo Stagg that was headed toward matrimony."

It was evident that Stella had found two loves of her life: A game and a man who coached it. It did not happen right away, though. Sixty-five years after that first meeting, when Stella was asked, "Did Mr. Stagg fall for you right away?" she replied, "Gollies no! There were too many other girls at the university."

Andy Wyant: Stagg's Polyphemus

During the U of C's second football season in 1893, Andy Wyant served as Chicago's first elected team captain. He was an imposing 6' 3" tall, with long hair and a big moustache. He was nicknamed "Polyphemus" after the giant Cyclops of Greek mythology.

Andy Wyant was a remarkable player, a true Maroon stalwart and played every minute of every U of C football game from 1892 through 1894: 73 consecutive games, including the grueling 23-game season of 1894. (He went on to serve as a Baptist minister, then become a prominent physician and served with distinction in the Red Cross during both World War I and World War II. He was inducted into the College Football Hall of Fame in 1962.).

With eight new recruits, Stagg retired as a player, except for one contest. Just before the game with Purdue, both of Chicago's quarterbacks were injured. So, Stagg, at the age of 31, played in a college football game one last time.

Andy Wyant later said of Stagg's last appearance as a player, "It was a road game which turned out to be extremely rough. Purdue had not yet been defeated on its home ground and had recently beaten Butler 96 to 0.

"The spectators behaved badly and criticized the umpire for faults that would have passed unnoticed had the struggle been lopsided. At one point in the game, slugging was prominent. Finally, the local prosecuting attorney literally walked out on the field and loudly informed both teams that the Tippecanoe County grand jury was in session and he was ready to seek indictments of every man on either team for assault and battery."

It was a different situation when Chicago played a second game with Northwestern later that season. At Northwestern's request, Stagg refereed the game, since no one else was available to do so, and the play was friendly and clean. The score was tied, 6 to 6, at halftime, when the secretary of the university rushed into the Maroon dressing room and implored the Maroons to win because, "John D. Rockefeller's personal representative is here." Stagg's Maroons pleased Rockefeller by coming from behind to win, 22-14.

Eighteen ninety-three was also the year the Maroons acquired a permanent home field. "During the fall of 1892," said Stagg, "football games at the University of Chicago, when not played in Washington Park, were played at 39th Street and Wentworth Avenue because the University had no home grounds. This situation produced numerous difficulties. As a matter of fact, in the second

44

game we played at Washington Park in 1892, an unexpectedly large crowd of people showed up. It is difficult when there are no bleachers and people crowd the field to tell whether a man is on the field of play or whether he steps over the sideline.

"I started on an end run, and the crowd had come in a ways. I broke right through the crowd, where there also happened to be a mounted policeman on his horse. When he saw me coming, he headed his horse out of the way and down the field. Although I don't recall it at all, people insisted that I followed the mounted policeman and used him as interference. Someone later wrote a story about how I scored a touchdown by cleverly using a mounted policeman as a blocker."

Stagg, of course, knew he'd get no money from the university for a stadium, but he was at his most persuasive in appealing to a highly-successful retailer for help. "On April 3, 1893," wrote Stagg, "local merchant Marshall Field granted the use of the block he owned bounded by Ellis Avenue, 57th Street, Greenwood Avenue and 56th Street as an athletic field and subscriptions were invited in order to enclose the field with a high board fence. The John Spry Lumber Company made a donation of lumber. A total of $865.50 was raised against an expenditure of $1311.15 on the field." The rest, as usual, came out of Stagg's pocket and he personally directed a crew of students as they built wooden bleachers sufficient to hold 150 spectators.

"The first baseball game played on this site, which was fittingly named 'Marshall Field' was with the University of Virginia in the summer of 1893, in what was called the 'World's Fair Series'," added Stagg. "In preparing for that baseball season, I constructed the first indoor batting cage. It was suspended from the ceiling of the gymnasium and enclosed an area 70 feet x 30 feet (Stagg later adapted his invention of the batting cage to outdoor use)."

"All home football games in the fall of 1893 were played at Marshall Field," recalled Stagg. "It was no trouble at all selling tickets to a Thanksgiving Day game with Michigan, and they were very expensive for those days at 50 cents each."

The victory caused so much rejoicing that the team was put on a cart pulled by sixty men to President Harper's house. Harper spoke to the crowd and saluted the players, saying, "Gentlemen of the football team, I am proud of you. You have won a glorious victory. I hope you may do as well in life." It also pleased John D. Rockefeller, who immediately dispatched a gift of $10,000 to the university.

"As a way of increasing attendance for games scheduled during cold weather months," continued Stagg, "I arranged an indoor football game at a neutral site when we played Northwestern at Tattersall's (a covered pavilion on 16th Street used for horse shows and boxing matches) on December 16, 1893 and won, 22 to 14. Over the course of the next four seasons, we played three more indoor games -- one with Notre Dame at Tattersall's and two against Michigan in the Chicago Coliseum. Chicago won all four indoor contests."

"An outgrowth of these indoor games was the huddle," wrote Stagg. "Before the 1896 Chicago vs. Michigan game in the Coliseum, I told the Chicago team to group together before each play to get the signals, since the reverberations from the cheering made it difficult to hear. This was done throughout that game and also throughout the game with Michigan in the Coliseum in 1897, but I didn't follow up and use this plan for outdoors. Many years later, in 1922, Bob Zuppke introduced the use of the huddle in outdoor games. In point of fact, though, the very first use of the huddle was by Gallaudet, an eastern college for the deaf, as a means of facilitating the 'sign language' they used for communicating plays to each other."

Stagg also noted that, "1893 was also the year I collaborated with my former Yale teammate Henry Williams on a book: 'A Scientific and Practical Treatise on American Football for Schools and Colleges' -- the first book on American football to include diagrams of plays. I diagramed 41 of the 55 plays in the book. Walter Camp had written the first book on American football, then former Princeton player Edgar Allan Poe wrote one in 1891, then we were next, but Camp and Poe didn't include any plays in their books." Stagg and Williams' collaboration was the first instance of a "play book" for any sport. Stagg had actually started making diagrams of plays in 1890 while at Springfield. This seemingly innocuous innovation had far-reaching implications and changed the face of all sports. It transformed the "team captain" into a "coach" by elevating the process of strategizing in athletic competition from mere on-the-field instructions to actual learning situations.

The appeal of University of Chicago football as a spectator attraction was enhanced in 1894 when new stands at the west and north ends of the field increased seating capacity and made the proceedings more orderly. "We again played Michigan at Marshall Field on Thanksgiving Day and were not only able to charge 50 cents admission," recalled Mr.Stagg, "but also sold 'carriage stand' tickets for even more. Allowing spectators to watch the game from carriages, however, led to an unfortunate incident which had nothing to do with football. Four young men drove onto the field on a two-wheeled trap. The horses became frightened and ran away; throwing out the men and smashing the cart. One of the young men wound up with his arm in a sling."

After only two years on The Midway, much had happened to Stagg, but even bigger things were on the horizon. The University of Chicago would at last field a squad to be reckoned with and he would marry the girl who would become the love of his life.

THE RISE AND FALL OF THE "MONSTERS OF THE MIDWAY"

After two difficult years, Stagg was hopeful of Chicago's football team finally becoming competitive with any opponent on their schedule; optimism fueled by the arrival of several talented new players, including quarterback Frank Hering, who had graduated from Williamsport, Pennsylvania's high school with the highest scholastic average in the school's history. "Hering was my quarterback in 1894, and the first quarterback to line up directly behind a center in a semi-erect stance to receive a snap, as in what is referred to as the 'T-Formation'," wrote Stagg. "He was the first man I ever encountered with large enough hands to able to throw a football like a baseball. Because of this, I was able to employ a backward pass on kickoff returns. Hering would catch the ball, then fire it out laterally to an end or a halfback."

Hering began playing quarterback for the U of C in 1893. He transferred to Bucknell in 1895. The next year, 1896, Frank Hering arrived at the University of Notre Dame to play quarterback, but by 1898, he had taken on the additional responsibilities of directing the entire athletic department, coaching the football and baseball teams and introducing basketball to Notre Dame. He was Notre Dame's first paid football coach. He earned the title of the "Father of Notre Dame Football" for his success in expanding the football program from an intramural activity to a full-fledged intercollegiate sport. In tribute to Hering's contributions, Knute Rockne instituted the "Hering Award", given to the most improved player during spring practice.   One of the recipients of the Hering Award was Notre Dame's legendary coach Frank Leahy.

Frank Hering has been recognized by the Fraternal Order of Eagles as the "Father of Mother's Day".   He gave speeches promoting the establishment of a national holiday for mothers as far back as February,1904.   He also used his position with the Eagles to sponsor America's first workman's compensation law and old age pension law.

While a member of the Notre Dame faculty in his later years, Frank Hering became known for his outreach programs in South Bend, Indiana, including the establishment of "Hering House": A civic center for South Bend's African-American community.

Lon and Stella become teammates for life

It was also during this time that Stagg got to know Stella Robertson, the young coed from New York who called him "Lon", and he became devoted to her.   He discovered that she played basketball and tennis for Chicago's women's teams, as well as enjoying recreational sports, such as bicycling, and that she was interested in physiology and had hopes of becoming a physician.   Stella was deeply religious and, despite a fourteen-year difference in their ages, she and Lon not only had a great deal in common; they were true soul mates.   They announced their engagement in the spring of 1894.

Lon had previously committed to working at a YMCA camp in Wisconsin, while Stella went back east for the summer; so they weren't able to spend much time together, but they wrote to each other on a daily basis.   If either of them went to the mailbox and found no letter, their heart would drop, then they would sit right down and write to the other about how disappointed they were. What they wrote about wasn't nearly as important as just seeing to it that they sent each other a daily letter. In the case of Lon and Stella, absence truly made the heart grow fonder, and the letter writing became a lifelong habit for them which they found great comfort in. By then, they had decided to marry before the year was out, spend a year in study abroad; then return back east; so that they both could go to medical school.

Even the truest of love comes to a crossroads. An obstacle arises that tests the love and a tough decision must be made. This happened to Lon and Stella less than three weeks after Stella's eighteenth birthday. On August 26, 1894, Lon wrote to her explaining how things had suddenly changed.

"My own Darling. This is my second letter today. I wrote you this A.M. that I would write you about the new circumstances which possibly may change our recent plan of getting married next month. I am sorry to have to say that we may have to wait, for I have had a strong feeling of satisfaction, which I thought was founded on reason, in contemplating an early marriage and a chance to work together unmolested by the 'cutting into the whole', as you so aptly put it.

"I went to see President Harper recently and I waited till 11:30 P.M. to see him. He was tired and sleepy and wanted me to wait until the next afternoon, but I begged a few minutes because I had spent 4 hours on the three different occasions waiting in vain when I had tried to see him. So, he sat down and talked with me for 10 or 15 minutes about our affairs. He asked me about our plans and I told him of our recent plan -- to get married next month and study here until Christmas and then go to Boston. He then told me that he did not think that it was the best plan; that he thought that I ought to let you go through and graduate, then get married and settle down in a home. Meantime, that I study and by the time I was ready to take an M.D., they would have a medical school here from where I could take it.

"I asked why, and he said for three reasons. First, that if I married you, it would hurt my influence among the profs and among the students. Second, that it would be bad for you. That you ought to have a chance to develop. That I was a strong character and old and set in my ways. That you ought to have a chance to develop your own ideas, so that you would not be a slave to my thought. Third, that it would hurt the cause of education and hurt the university.

"I told him that in the first one I disagreed with him because I had very little influence in the faculty and that I never should have until I impressed them with my intellect.

"He disclaimed the idea that I had no influence, but I fought it out with him and told him that I had been used as a sacrifice for the university: That my reputation had been inflated for the sake of drawing students to the university to such a degree that, of course, when people came to know me they could not fail to give me a fall, for my reputation was unreal. He denies this, but I am certain that he knew it was true, as it certainly is. At the very beginning of the university, I was invited to dinners and to give speeches on all occasions when the other 'big people' spoke. Of course, I could not meet the reputation which I had been given, and so my influence decreased. I gave it to him straight, Stella dear, for I have felt that I had been put on a pedestal and had been unduly heralded and inflated so much so that I could not fail to fall. I know that he knew that he had used me as a sacrifice for the university.

"Well, little one, I told him that I was willing for the sake of the university to have been made a sacrifice. The only way that I can ever get influence and reputation now, I told him, was to have the profs respect me for my intellect. They certainly will give me little respect for my muscle, and I don't want it, darling.

"I told him that the second point is only my concern and the third is of little or no consequence. It is of consequence to me to have you develop, Darling, yet I disagreed with him. If I am set in my ways now, I told him, I shall be more so at the end of another two years and I shall have an effect on you anyway.

"I want you to know, my precious, precious Darling, that I do not want my own way for the sake of having it; that unless you can see things the way I see them after a calm reasoning of the matter, I do not want to force them on you. I do earnestly want to do the right and best thing always, whether it be my wish or not.

"He also said that if we get married as we plan to, that would be a most anomalous position for you -- you would be a prof's wife and a student at the same time. At the receptions you would sometimes come in with students and sometimes with the faculty. But I told him that we could fix that, all right, by not appearing. He didn't like that because he wants us present.

"He told me that if it were anybody else of my rank or lower that did as I proposed, he should ask for their resignation. But he told me he would not do that with me because he valued me so highly and because he believed in me, etc., etc. On four different occasions during the conversation he came to, 'but you should do what you think best and I'll stand by you.'

"I told him that it would not make a bit of difference with me if he did fire me and if I felt it was best to get married now, I'll do it.

"I was perfectly calm as was he, only I let him know that I wanted to do the right and best thing and I did not care a cent for the consequences. He then gave me a lot of talk about my being invaluable and that I had done a great deal for the university, but I only wish he would leave out his policy words when he talks to me. Then he said, 'Why don't you get married and take off for a year?' I told him I didn't think that was a good idea.

"You see, Darling, I do not think that I ought to lose whatever glory can come from our football season this year. For two years, I have worked hard to get a winning team together and now it looks as though we might have one. If I leave, they might not win and, if that happens, I should be criticized for leaving. So, it is better that I do stay here this fall.

"I must close now and hurry to supper and then to a mission meeting, but whatever we decide, my precious, precious Darling, I love you with all my heart."

Affectionately, Lonnie.

Contending with all the negativity and distractions involved in starting an entire athletic department from scratch, not to mention his impending marriage and meeting his in-laws for the first time, began to take a toll on Stagg. On September 3, 1894, he wrote Stella, "I am sick of all this hurly burly -- all of this rush after money -- all of this disbelief in people -- all of this criticism whether of work or of character. The fine sensibilities and graces of a person's nature, the delicate expressions of one's life, all pass by unnoticed and the most beautiful characters are maligned and subjected to criticism and doubtful questioning. Such it has seemed to me for a long time is the way of the Chicago world and I hate it with all the intensity of my nature and I would not stay here for a day did I not feel called to throw in my life to help change this boorishness -- this ugly hateful spirit of unappreciation of the higher and finer things of living -- this devilish greed after money -- this detestible disregard in cultivating courtesy and kindness and generosity of spirit and giving for others' good. Oh it is easy to explain, I suppose, but it is not easy to stem the tide."

Each passing day became more and more intense for him. Only Stella could understand what was going on in his mind and in his heart, and he realized he would never find anyone else who would be able to do that. Things had gone way beyond what could be solved through written words, and only deeds mattered.

"Mr. Stagg had planned to meet Stella's family a week later," related Dr. Marc Jantzen. "He took a train to Buffalo, with a planned connection of 20 miles to Stella's town of Albion. But it was four hours before the local was scheduled to leave.

"Years later, when Mr. Stagg related this to my wife and I in our living room, he said that, 'I just had to see that girl! I didn't want to wait that long, so I bought a bicycle and bicycled to Stella's town.'

"They spent their time together during the next day or two bicycling around the countryside and playing tennis. One morning during a tennis match, Mr. Stagg said, 'Stella, let's get married!'

"'When?' she asked.

"'This afternoon.'

"And so they were married that afternoon -- September 10, 1894. Stella's mother scurried around for a minister and invited a few neighbors. Then, it was back to the University of Chicago in time for football practice, and no honeymoon."

Though their actions might seem impulsive, their wedding day resulted from the couple's long discussions about the direction they would take. With all the changeableness and uncertainty they were forced to wade through in planning their future, their decision all came down to the fact that Lon had come as far as he had all because of a pledge he made to his Master to serve young men by being a coach. If Lon broke the promise he made to his players of being there for them when they needed him most, he would be abandoning his mission and betraying all he had professed. How could a woman like Stella love that kind of man?

Where he and Stella were was where they were meant to be, and where they were meant to fight the good fight -- not in Europe or back east. If he truly wanted respect for his brain as well as his brawn, it was up to him to see that the game he coached was respected, and that being a coach would be regarded as a worthy profession. Stagg realized he was the vanguard in the development of football. He carried the fledgling sport on his shoulders and was up to him to take it where it had to go. For the game to ever enjoy wide appeal, it would have to be something that was fun for all. If he left Chicago at that point, football would never be fun for his players. He would break his players' hearts; because they would never have known how good they could have been, and they would hate him for the rest of their lives for empty promises and for his absence preventing them from becoming all that they might.

She asked if their getting married would jeopardize his position with the university, and he said it wouldn't, because, "President Harper didn't object to our getting married this September, he simply said that he did not think that it was the wisest course to follow." Lon's decision was easy to make, for he had no choice but to do the right thing. The right thing was the best thing, and he had promised Stella that all he ever wanted was what was best for them. Stella also had no choice, for all she really wanted was to be Lon's wife.

Over the course of their years together, there was never a doubt that, outside of their religion, the biggest thing in their lives was their marriage. Their lifetime together would become a testament of devotion to the University of Chicago and to the game of football. They had three children -- Amos Alonzo, Jr., Ruth and Paul. They all graduated from the University of Chicago. Both Amos Alonzo, Jr. and Paul played football for their father at Chicago, then went into coaching; but not before their father counseled them that, "No man ought to go into coaching except for service. He must catch the vision of the great work to which he feels called and the tremendous opportunities for service to boys and young men, and be inspired to personal self improvement and to high ideals of personal living in order to be worthy of his calling."

Stella later wrote of their earliest years together, "When I married Lon, I was surprised that he didn't have more money on hand than he did. I don't remember the details, but I remember the feeling of surprise. I knew that he had helped his folks and I knew that he had sent his sister Pauline to Vassar, but, though he had some investments, his bank account was low.

"We sure had lean years in those early days. As an associate professor, Lon's salary was only $2500. We even put off our honeymoon, and that later turned out to be a long trip to California with the football team."

That trip took place after Chicago had concluded its 1894 season and Stagg described it as a "transcontinental football pilgrimage". "Leland Stanford Junior University (now called Stanford University) and the University of Chicago played a unique contest that year," stated Mr. Stagg. "It was unique not just because of the youth of both universities and because Walter Camp coached that Stanford team, but because it was the first trip of a football team across the Rocky Mountains. The audacity of it may be realized when you consider that there was scant money for such a trip.

"Negotiations were opened with Stanford, who made an unprecedented offer -- a guarantee of $1000 and 75% of the net receipts -- for a game on Christmas Day, 1894. Stanford was willing to assume the entire guarantee because, at first, they stipulated that we could play only that game against their team during our visit, and thus ensure a sizeable gate. This stipulation was later removed because the Reliance Athletic Club, which had an option on the best exhibition grounds in San Francisco for Christmas Day, refused the use of the grounds to Stanford unless Stanford gave them the privilege of a game with the University of Chicago on New Year's Day. Stanford, therefore, withdrew their objections, and we then had two games to play.

"Besides the Reliance Athletic Club, the University of California also wished a game. I left the long distance negotiations up to the Californians for settlement by sending them the following wire on the day we left, 'Will play the University of California or the Reliance Athletic Club on New Year's Day for $1000.00 guarantee with privilege of three-fourths the gate receipts. Will play the University of California or the Reliance Athletic Club on Jan. 3 for $500.00 guarantee with privilege of three-fourth receipts. Settle among yourselves.'

"The final result was that Stanford played Chicago in San Francisco on Christmas Day and at Los Angeles December 29th and the Reliance Athletic Club played Chicago at San Francisco on New Year's Day, 1895. The games in San Francisco were played on the Haight Street Grounds, which seated about 5000 people. Tickets for the Stanford game there cost $1.50, with $1.00 for general admission."

"Great enthusiasm was displayed by the Chicago boys for the trip," recalled Mr. Stagg. "I held President Harper to his promise of three years before regarding a 'palace car and a vacation' and the University agreed to underwrite all expenses and arranged for a private railroad car, called the 'Georgia', a combination dining car and sleeper, to be used for the trip. A private chef went along to provide meals for the team and the men looked forward to a luxurious trip to the coast. The party consisted of 16 players, myself and my bride of four months.

"The private car, however, proved to be a 'joke on us'. Instead of luxurious appointments, the car was a derelict; a worn-out railroad car formerly used by traveling minstrel shows, and many times during the trip it seemed doubtful it would make it back to Chicago. The first night out was truly 'explosive', when the upper berths collapsed. But what was lacking in luxurious appointments was made up for by the culinary efforts of the chef. Thick juicy steaks, and plenty of them, were enjoyed by all.

"As San Francisco approached, embarrassment over the shabbiness of the car caused us to transfer to regular Pullmans in which we arrived to meet our California hosts, and we also took regular Pullmans from San Francisco to Los Angeles. When we arrived, the Californians kidded us about being Chicagoans who brought their own river water to drink.

"We played the first contest with snap and vim. Chicago won that game with Stanford handily, 24 to 4. As Walter Camp had aided in the coaching of Stanford during their fall training, the game attracted interest as a contest between the coaching of two Yale men.

"At Los Angeles, the weather was rainy and the atmosphere humid. The second game with Stanford played at Los Angeles was won by Stanford, 12 to 0. Our share of the receipts was a third of what it had been in San Francisco, since the Los Angeles Amateur Athletic Club's involvement resulted in a three-way split, rather than 75-25." Football historians consider the December 29th Chicago vs. Stanford contest to be the genesis of the modern-day college bowl game -- two college teams playing a post-season contest promoted by an outside organization at a neutral warm weather site.

"We played another game in Los Angeles, with the Reliance Athletic Club, and lost, 6 to 0," continued Stagg. "Our share of the gate helped to balance our accounts, though. On the way back, we played the Y.M.C.A. of Salt Lake City, Utah in snow and slush. It was a very unpleasant affair and brought in a small amount of money.

We finished slightly in the red -- about $135 -- and that probably would have been avoided if we hadn't experienced trouble with our railroad car.

"Because of the Georgia's seventy-foot length, we discovered during the trip back that it couldn't be parked and locked up in snow sheds. This forced our traveling party to sleep in the rail car rather than a hotel. The wood burning stove wasn't up to such extended use, became overheated, and started a fire. Faster action took place from the players than in the Stanford game and that saved the coach and its occupants.

"The car was laid up for repairs in Laramie. While there, some of the players went hunting and killed two jackrabbits. These were served on board and enjoyed by those who liked the taste of wild game. Stella and I, though, stuck with the steaks."

"Stagg must have really loved the boys on that team," said Andy Wyant. "Did you ever hear of any other man who took 16 fellows along with him on his honeymoon?"

After that long trip to California, what would become the most famous football coaching team -- Mr. and Mrs. Amos Alonzo Stagg -- was forged; and they would go on as true teammates for seventy years. Fred Long Farley, the Pacific "Family Poet", put it this way:

TO STELLA STAGG

He made his peace with God when he was young
And paid Him homage with the work he chose
No ordinary man, he pledged his tongue
His sharp young mind, trained strength.

On
these arose

Quick fame, a further challenge for his store
Of innovating gifts, to channel all
His native energies.   His fame grew more --
Made him the earth's Evangelist of Ball.

His strong and earthy wisdom shook
Strange unity into a team.   And soon,
They say, he loved his boys so much he took
Some twenty players on his honeymoon.

The friendly gracious lady at his side,
No "gridiron widow", still is Football's Bride

Stagg's innovations in other sports

"In 1896," said Stagg, "I came up with the idea of using a succession of quick 'wind sprints' for conditioning purposes.   Before that time, only distance runs were used. That was also the year I adapted my invention of an indoor batting cage for outdoor use.   It was made of wire netting fastened to upright posts set firmly in the ground, 70 feet long and 10 feet wide."

In January of that same year, Stagg's University of Chicago basketball team played a University of Iowa squad coached by H.F. Kallenberg, a close friend of Stagg's from their days at Springfield College.   Their game in Iowa City was the first time a basketball game was conducted in a way which would be recognizable today -- five players to a side and with a referee.   Previously, basketball had been played with seven to nine players on each side and the players called the fouls themselves. Basketball had been invented by James Naismith, a Canadian who played football for Stagg at Springfield; but the Grand Old Man was a big part of it. As a matter of fact, he played in the very first game of what Naismith had originally named "basket football". The *San Francisco Chronicle's* Art Rosenbaum wrote of how Stagg "once remarked that he had told Naismith how high to put the first peach basket (peach baskets were used before hoops and nets were developed)." What Rosenbaum alluded to was Stagg's suggestion that the basket be ten feet above the ground, rather than Naismith's original plan of eight feet.

Dr. Marc Jantzen revealed another connection Stagg had to Naismith and to the beginnings of the "roundball game" when he said, "Chancellor Snow of the University of Kansas came to Mr. Stagg asking if he knew of a man to fill a unique position -- a combination athletic director and chaplain. Stagg told him, 'I know just the man for you, James Naismith.' In addition, Stagg invented the 'three-on-one fast break' in December 1920."

"Double A's" contributions to basketball were recognized when he was among the first group of inductees for the Basketball Hall of Fame; for what would basketball be without ten-foot-high baskets and the fast break?

Perhaps the most far-reaching of Mr. Stagg's athletic innovations, though, was the idea of an "intercollegiate conference"; an alternative to the "leagues" and "athletic associations" which previously governed football with little, if any, control exerted by the academic institutions themselves. The "intercollegiate conference" would not only establish and maintain eligibility standards for its members' athletes, but it would also place control of its members' athletic competition in the hands of faculty members of the member institutions. It took a couple of years for Stagg and President Harper to find a staunch ally in Purdue's president James H. Smart, who was in a position to bring this concept to reality. At Smart's urging, presidents of seven midwestern colleges held a meeting in Chicago in January,1895 which led to the formation of "The Intercollegiate Conference of Faculty Representatives", popularly known as "The Big Ten". Stagg was among the very first group of duly-appointed Big Ten faculty representatives, but the only one who was also a coach. His idea has since become the pattern copied by most college conferences.

Clarence Herschberger: Stagg's first All-American

"Clarence Herschberger was from Peoria, Illinois," wrote Stagg, "and had entered the University of Chicago in the fall term of 1894. He was then eighteen years of age. He came out for football and at once exhibited superior talent for the game. At that time, experienced football players were few in number, and 'Herschie' was one of those few. While not a large man --158 pounds -- he was gifted athletically. In addition to football, he was a classy baseball player and a good all-around track man. He was the only Chicago athlete to ever win 13 letters.

"His athletic reputation was greatest in football, and he was the first player west of the Allegheny Mountains to be selected on Walter Camp's All-American team. He was an exceptional punter. He consistently punted fifty to fifty-five yards, and he could make his kicks fade away from the return man as they dropped to the ground, which bothered anyone trying to catch one of his punts.

"His mother objected, though, and wouldn't allow him to play. So, in 1895, he refused to go to college and stayed home. That fall while hunting, he had the misfortune of wounding himself in the hand. After figuring there were more dangerous things her son could be doing after all, his mother gave her consent to his playing football and he returned to the university in the spring. "He won the 1896 Chicago-Michigan game with a 40-yard drop kick, making the final score 7 to 6. When we beat Michigan in 1897, 21-12, fifteen of our 21 points came from Herschberger's place kicks." Herschberger was the first player to use the "Statue of Liberty" play.

"Herschberger had become so clever in his kicking by 1898 that I had him practice striking the top of the ball, or 'topping' it, as he kicked off," said Stagg. "This caused the ball to bounce crazily for 10 yards, then Herschberger could recover it himself. We sprang that play against Pennsylvania in Philadelphia that year and 'Herschie' recovered his own kick for a net gain of eighteen yards. Walter Camp saw that Penn-Chicago game and, because of that performance, placed Herschberger on his All-American team -- the first 'western' player to be so honored." It's interesting to note how impressed Camp was, even though Chicago lost, 23-11.

Herschberger, however, wasn't always a joy to Coach Stagg. He blamed Herschberger and the Maroons' team captain and quarterback Walter Kennedy for losing the 1897 Big Ten Championship.

"Herschberger and Walter Kennedy, who were close friends, unbeknown to me staged a contest to see who could put on the most weight in one sitting," recalled Mr. Stagg.

"Herschie gained seven pounds and Kennedy seven and a quarter pounds. Herschie had eaten thirteen eggs during that contest and, as a result, had gastric fever and could not play. I always felt that Herschie's indiscretion lost the Wisconsin game, and with it the championship, because he was an indispensable part of the team." Without Herschberger's kicking, Chicago lost, 23 to 8. It was their only loss in a 12-game season.

During the 1899 season, Stagg's players recognized the maturity, knowledge and judgment of their 37-year-old coach and began calling him the "Old Man" out of their fondness for him. Little did they realize how enduring their nickname for him was to become. Chicago was 12-0-2 that year, ranked fourth in the nation and the best in the midwest. Three of Stagg's players were named All-American by Walter Camp: Quarterback Walter Kennedy, halfback Frank Slaker and end Ralph Hamill. One of the season's highlights was Chicago's 17-6 win over Percy Haughton's Cornell team. Another occurred on October 4, 1899 when Chicago played Notre Dame for the last time and won, 23 to 6; giving them a clean sweep over the Fighting Irish.

"Then on December 9, 1899," added Stagg, "Chicago played Wisconsin at Madison in a post season game. We scored a touchdown on a new play of mine -- a 'delayed buck'. The quarterback faked to a halfback as he crossed diagonally in front of the fullback, but gave the ball to the fullback, who made a buck between center and guard for a four-yard touchdown."

Stagg's pioneering efforts give impetus to our Olympic movement

With his lifelong passion for running, it was only natural that "Double A" liked coaching track second only to football, and much more than baseball. In fact, baseball was the first sport he stopped coaching as the University of Chicago grew and enlarged its athletic staff. The formation of the Western Conference in 1896 contributed to track becoming a major intercollegiate sport, and Stagg coached the first Maroon track team that year. Under Stagg's coaching, Chicago won four outdoor and three indoor championships and when Mr. Stagg retired from track in 1928, he was the oldest track coach in the country in point of service. He developed a knack of producing great quarter and half-milers. His greatest runner competed just before World War I: Binga Dismond, a powerful young man from very modest surroundings who worked his way through the University of Chicago and would become the first African-American track star. Stagg was also a member of the U.S. Olympic Committee from 1906 to 1932. He coached our country's 400 and 800 meter runners and the 1600 meter relay team at the Paris Olympics in 1924.

Mr. Stagg's system of developing track stars boiled down to just simply hard work. He was tolerant of many things, but had neither time nor sympathy for any athlete who wouldn't train. Physical conditioning was as much a gospel to Stagg as if it came directly from the Bible.

One of Chicago's star runners once complained to Stagg that he had gotten little out of college and he had no idea what he was going to do to earn a living.

"I think you got a lot out of college," the Grand Old Man replied. "You know how to wear clothes. You know which knife and fork to use at the proper time. Don't worry about making a living. That's easy. Just work hard and be honest. That's all you ought to learn in college.

"If you want to do a lot for your country, you ought to try being a coach and work with youngsters as they grow up."

Stagg played an important role in bringing American collegiate track to the level of world-class competition. "After several years of corresponding with Baron Pierre de Coubertin, who was organizing the Olympics," continued Stagg, "I persuaded President Harper during the spring of 1900 to have the university join me in borrowing $2000 from a bank to send an eight-man track team to represent the United States at the Paris Olympic Games."

In accompanying that Olympic squad, Stagg faced many risks attached to trans-Atlantic voyages in those days. Mindful of this, Stagg wrote a letter to his fourteen-month-old son in the event something untoward happened. It read:

June 23, 1900

To my son, Amos Alonzo Stagg, Jr.:

You are only a little fellow now -- a trifle over 14 months old -- but I have loved you so dearly since you came that it has been on my mind to write you a letter in the event of my being taken away at any time before I have had a chance to tell you many things which you need to know.

Your father wants his Boy first of all to love, protect and care for his Mother, giving to her the same kind of measure of love and devotion which she has given you.

Second, your father wants his Boy to be sincere, honest and upright. Be your true self always. Hate dishonesty and trickery no matter how big and how great the thing desired may be.

Third, your father wants you to have a proper independence of thought. Think matters out for yourself always where it relates to your own conduct and act honestly afterwards.

Fourth, your father wants you to be an American in democracy. Treat everybody with courtesy and as your equal until he proves his unworthiness to be so treated. The man and the soul are what count -- not wealth, not family, not appearance.

Fifth, your father wants you to abhor evil. No curiosity, no imagination, no conversation, no story, no reading which suggests impurity of life is worthy of your thought or attention and I beg you never to yield for an instant, but to turn your thought to something good and helpful.

Sixth, train yourself to be master of yourself, of your thought and imagination and temper and passion and appetite and of your body. Hold all absolutely under your will. Allow no thought nor imagination, nor passion, nor

69

appetite to injure your mind or body. Your father has never used intoxicating liquors, nor tobacco, nor profane language. He wants his Boy to be like him in this regard.

Seventh, your father wants his Boy enthusiastic and earnest in all of his interests, his sports, his studies, his work; and he wants him always to keep an active, actual participation in each so long as he lives. It is my judgment that one's life is most healthy and most successful when lived out on such a basis.

Eighth, your father wants his son to love God as He is revealed to him; which after all will be the revelation of all that I have said and left unsaid of good to you, my precious Boy.

Affectionately,
Your Father

Mr. Stagg's coaching salary and plans for financial security

"Lon became a professor in 1900," recalled Stella, And his promotion in academic rank meant that his salary went from $2500 to $4000. Before President Harper died of cancer in 1906, he raised Lon's salary to $6,000, where it remained for 14 years.

"1924, when Lon's salary became $8000, was the start of the best investment period of our lives. Two years later, we invested in some small orange groves in Orlando, Florida. It cost us an average of $781 per year to operate them, but we considered it a future retirement home. Little did we know where we would be actually spending our last years."

The Big Ten's first great rivalry: Chicago vs. Michigan

Fielding Yost joined the Big Ten coaching fraternity in 1900 and his years with the Michigan Wolverines would contribute an important chapter to the Big Ten's story. The following year,1901, was the start of Michigan's five-season domination of college football. Stagg and Yost came from decidedly different backgrounds, which resulted in them holding different views of college football. Rather than having "Fight the good fight' as a motto, Yost would say, "Follow the searchlights and step over the bodies." His players were known to have said to opposing linemen, "Say, this play coming up is the same one we killed a man with last year."

Similar to Stagg, Yost came up the hard way. He grew up living in a log cabin, first worked as a deputy marshal in rowdy mining towns and later earned money for college by teaching in one-room schools and laboring in oil fields. At twenty-four, he entered the University of West Virginia's law school and while there played in the first football game he ever saw. He weighed 200 pounds, good size for then, and was a starter for three teams at one time. He soon gained a reputation as a man "who could play football all day and talk it all night."

Early on, he was captivated by football because he believed it was a way out of the West Virginia mining towns; so he decided to seek his fortune by becoming a coach and started his coaching career at a tiny Ohio Wesleyan in 1897. He then drifted to Nebraska and Kansas, winning conference titles at each of those schools, before carrying a 24-3-1 record into his fourth season and fourth job at Stanford. His Stanford team was 7 and 2 his only year there, and that was a year he also coached Stanford's freshman team, San Jose State, San Francisco's Lowell High School and "California Ukiah" -- an independent team. He was forced to leave Stanford when all Pacific Coast universities adopted a rule requiring their schools hire only coaches who were graduates of that school. So, he applied for the job at Illinois, but found it filled; then hooked on at Michigan. He always believed that the mark of excellence for a football team was how dominant they were and, after being snubbed while out on the west coast, he was determined to assemble the most dominant squad ever seen.

Fielding Yost spoke in the quaint dialect of his native Appalachian region and at practices, he'd exhort his players with, "Hurry up! Hurry up! If ye cain't hurry up, make way for someone who can!" If a big player loafed, Yost would chastise him with," Y'know, lad, God made ye big! He made ye muscles strong! He gave ye good health! And you're playin' like a wooden Indian in front of a cigar store! If I would put ye in a greenhouse and gave ye an axe and a shotgun, ye couldn't get aout! How do ye expect to fight for Meesheegan!" With his "survival of the fittest" mentality, Yost insisted that his "Eleven Iron Men of Meesheegan" play entire games without substitution, or any allowance for injury.

He was extremely competitive and didn't mind occasionally cutting corners. Yost was also an unashamed ham, a born exhibitionist and a rare person who could boast and still be liked for it. That quality served him well when the Wolverines went on their terror from 1901-1905. His team became known as the "Point-A-Minute Dynasty".

72

They had a 56-game unbeaten streak during that period and scored 2821 points to their opponents' 42, at a time when touchdowns only counted for five points. Yost relished running up scores and his Wolverines blistered Buffalo 128-0 and West Virginia 130-0.

Michigan played Stanford in the very first Rose Bowl -- New Year's Day, 1902 -- and butchered the Stanford Indians (now known as Stanford Cardinal) so badly, 49-0, that Stanford ran out of able-bodied men and the game had to be called off with seven minutes left. The carnage Michigan inflicted did not give southern Californians the sort of game they had hoped to watch, so it was 14 years before another Rose Bowl was played.

During the Wolverines' skein, only two teams gave them any kind of a struggle. Stagg's Chicago team scored 12 points against Michigan in 1904, losing 22-12, and Minnesota played Yost's "Mighty Men of Michigan" to a 6-6 tie in 1903. With only those two close calls, it appeared Michigan just might never lose.

While Yost was enjoying Michigan's winning streak, Mr. Stagg was contributing more sports innovations. He recalled, "When faced with a problem in scheduling practices because classes were being held so late that, by the time the football practices could begin, it was too dark to see anything; I painted the football white to make it easier to see it. For years and years after that, white or yellow-colored footballs were used by teams all over the country for night games. Later, I enclosed a section of the practice field with electric lights." He also established the "Order of the C" in 1902, which resulted in his awarding the first varsity letters and in the process creating the very first letterman's club. When Bartlett Gymnasium was erected in 1903, the plans included an indoor swimming pool. The idea was considered impractical at first, but it was made possible through Stagg's invention of troughs constructed around the sides of the pool to handle overflow and keep flotsam to a minimum.

As far as the performance of the football team was concerned, Chicago's 1901 season ended 5-5-2 (They fell to seventh place in the conference.) The "experts'" 1902 prognostications for the Maroons weren't favorable. Fielding Yost bluntly stated, "There are five great teams in the west this year; and Chicago isn't one of them." A positive factor, though, was that Stagg's manpower worries were finally over. His teams had grown to the point where they actually had reserves, although they were more like bench warmers than actual prospective starters. Some of the reserves weren't good enough to ever play in a game, but they still found enjoyment in being part of the team. Another positive was that all of the Maroons were also aided by all of their games in 1902 being home contests. Chicago shocked the football world by going 11-1 that season -- Big Ten runners up and ranked third in the nation.

The saga of Robert "Tiny" Maxwell

A big factor in that team's success was Robert Maxwell. A native of Chicago, Robert W. "Tiny" Maxwell graduated from Englewood High School. He began playing college football at the University of Chicago in 1902 for Amos Alonzo Stagg. At 6' 4" and 240 pounds, he also boxed and set school hammer and shot-put records. Maxwell played guard at Chicago in 1902.

Maxwell only played one year at Chicago before transferring to Swarthmore College. In addition to playing guard on Swarthmore's team, he was a track star, participating in discus and hammer throw. The versatile Maxwell was also a Shakespearean actor, and a song writer.

During the 1905 season at Swarthmore, Maxwell made a major impact on the game of football as we know it today. At the end of a savage contest with Penn, in which he turned in his customary stellar performance, Maxwell's nose broken, his eyes swollen nearly shut, and his face closely resembled a rare steak covered with red sauce. A newspaper photo of his face so shocked President Theodore Roosevelt, that two days later, in a meeting with major college representatives, the president demanded that they "clean up football," or he'd ban the game outright.

The 1905 season had been the deadliest football season in history. Eighteen players died while playing in football games and 159 were seriously injured. Three months later, rules were changed to double the yardage required for a first down from five to ten, reduce playing time from seventy minutes to sixty minutes, add restrictions against roughing, establish a neutral zone on the line of scrimmage the length of the football, and to legalize the forward pass.

After a brief, professional career playing for such teams as the Massillon Tigers and Canton Bulldogs, Maxwell's career as a referee began when he was called at the last minute to fill in for an official who didn't show up. Because of his tremendous size, quickness, and knowledge of the rules, he was soon in demand for such major games as Harvard-Yale and Army-Navy.

In time, Maxwell's role as an official would influence football considerably. Walter Camp said Maxwell set the standard for fairness and competence. Maxwell's apartment near City Hall in Philadelphia became a gathering place for fellow officials. Out of their meetings grew the first formal association of football officials in the East.

Maxwell also became one of the rare players to make the leap from field to press box. In 1914, after a journalistic apprenticeship in as a reporter for the *Chicago Record-Herald*, he began writing a sports column for Philadelphia's *Public Ledger*. Two years later, he became Sports Editor of the *Evening Public Ledger*, a position he held until his death.

Early in the summer of 1922, Maxwell and some friends went for a countryside drive north of Philadelphia. While returning that night, Maxwell eyed a car stopped directly in front of him. As he changed lanes to pass, he ran head-on into a truck carrying Boy Scouts home from a picnic. A passenger in Maxwell's car recalls seeing him pinned beneath the wreckage as he yelled, "Help the others, I can wait!!"

Tiny spent the next few days in a hospital, having suffered seven broken ribs, a punctured lung, and a dislocated hip. Pneumonia developed and delirium soon followed. On the night of June 29th, 1922 he was visited by his neighbor and close friend Charles Heeb. Emerging from his delirium, he talked of packing his bags and going home. "Take two hours' sleep and I'll go with you," Heeb told him. " All right kid," replied Maxwell, "I'll go to sleep," and he did. He passed away peacefully.

Tiny Maxwell was thirty-seven when he died. Fifteen years later, in 1937, The Robert W. Maxwell Memorial Football Club was founded in Philadelphia by Maxwell's friend, Bert Bell (who owned the NFL's Philadelphia Eagles and later became commissioner of the National Football League), to present awards in his name and to promote football safety.

Walter Eckersall: Chicago's "Little Big Man"

Nineteen hundred and three was the year Stagg's brightest football star of all arrived on campus -- Walter Eckersall. Eckersall had played for nearby Hyde Park High School. In his senior year, he led them to a national high school championship when they beat Brooklyn Polytechnic, 105 to 0. Princeton made overtures to Eckersall and Michigan wanted him, but he decided on Chicago so he could live at home and play for Stagg.

"Eckersall was one of the smallest and lightest boys who ever played for me," said the Grand Old Man. "When he came to the University of Chicago in the fall of 1903, he weighed only 132 pounds stripped; but even at that light weight, he superseded the regular quarterback of the previous year and cinched the starting position as a freshman. During the three succeeding years of his eligibility, he made small increases in weight, until in his senior year he attained 143 pounds.

"Here was a boy who was always smaller than his comrades, and yet he never lacked courage. He didn't say, 'Oh, what's the use of trying! All the kids are bigger and stronger than I.' He kept right at it and studied the fundamentals of play: how to do each technique in the best way. He tried to do everything well and kept on

77

improving. He had the ambition to participate in various sports, and he became expert in baseball and track, as well as football. He studied the important skills in each of the sports he participated in and sought to improve himself in whatever skills were required. To accomplish this, he had to practice regularly and consistently.

"In his personal life and habits while he was in high school and college, he realized that, to make good, he had to get sleep regularly and not smoke or drink, nor indulge in late parties. He was eager and willing to make the sacrifice for the satisfaction of doing well.

"He proved without question that he was an earnest student of the fundamentals of the game. When he tackled, he always caught the runner at the knees and took his legs out from under him quickly. When he blocked, he got the opponent low. As a quarterback, he was quick and skillful in handling the ball. In carrying the ball, he was quick and fast and clever in dodging tacklers. In catching punts, he was fearless and sure-handed. In drop-kicking and punting, he was exceptionally good. In calling signals, he was strategic and commanding."

"Eckersall's great fame never went to his head," continued Mr. Stagg. "He was modest and unassuming, quick to give credit to his comrades and always a good sportsman.

"In the four years of Eckersall's playing career at the University of Chicago, he scored 208 points. Three of those years were played under the 'old rules' before the introduction of the forward pass. Seventy of the 208 points were scored on 14 touchdowns. One hundred sixteen were scored on field goals and seventeen from points after touchdowns.

"As a freshman in 1903, he drop-kicked three field goals against Wisconsin, at a time when field goals counted five points, and Milwaukee newspapers headlined the game: 'Eckersall 15, Wisconsin 6.' In the Chicago-Illinois game of 1905, Eckersall drop-kicked five field goals, and the next season booted another five against Nebraska."

Knute Rockne, Notre Dame's greatest coach, would credit Eckersall for inspiring him to devote himself to the sport of football. By watching Eckersall, Rockne could see the creative possibilities of the sport.

Walter Eckersall made many long runs, but his greatest was against Wisconsin in 1904, in a game played on a 110-yard field, when he took a kickoff and ran 106 yards for a touchdown. Years later, his teammate Leo DeTray often paid tribute to Eckersall's unselfishness when he would tell of all the times "Eckie" would call upon other Maroon players to carry the ball inside the five in sure touchdown situations.

Eckersall, unfortunately, flunked out of the U of C, but later won fame as a football referee at the same time that he was a renowned sports writer for the *Chicago Tribune*. With his reputation for honesty and integrity when it came to sports, he officiated in important games from coast to coast and was always in demand to work a game until the day of his untimely death. In the sports writing field, he specialized, of course, in football, but he also covered boxing and was one of the fathers of the Golden Gloves. Sadly, one day in 1930, Eckersall was found dead from a heart attack in his suite at the Chicago Athletic Club. He was only 43 years old.

At the time of Eckersall's passing, Mr. Stagg was called upon for a statement about his All-American. He wrote, "Walter Eckersall's most predominant characteristic was his modesty. He never wished to be made anything of, and he ran away from fulsome praise. He was a fine sportsman and generous. He was always ready to give credit where credit was due.

"In his playing, 'Eckie' was very intense and hard working, and he had no patience with a loafer.

"Eckie did not like to make speeches, but he always spoke well when he did make them. What he said had such a modest and genuine ring to it and with so much self effacement, along with a fine quality of feeling in his voice, that he easily won the admiration and approbation of everybody who heard him. He never talked long, but he always talked well.

"He was exceedingly loyal to his mother, who was his greatest champion."

Stagg takes a spill and suffers a lingering injury

While the arrival of such talented players as Eckersall enhanced Chicago's football fortunes, Stagg suffered a physical setback at this time which nearly put a stop to his coaching; for at 40, he was still scrimmaging with his players to demonstrate correct techniques. It was ironic that his passion for running contributed to his misfortune. "A lack of good judgment on my part caused me to attempt a running broad jump over some water with my four-year-old son in my arms," recalled Mr. Stagg. "I landed on my back and injured my sacroiliac. Luckily, Amos Alonzo, Jr. wasn't hurt." The pain defied relief. He was unable to tell from one day to another just how to sit or how to stand, or even be able to do anything. Stagg's affliction was diagnosed as sciatica and, as Stella Stagg recalled, "From 1903 to 1909, practically all of our money went to get Lon over it."

Stagg eventually found a measure of relief in hot baths. He would spend hours in his tub at home and he would also arrange to hold coaching clinics in such places as Florida and Arkansas, so he could bathe in the hot spring waters at nearby resorts. He would also take the entire family on winter vacations to such places as Miami. During one such trip, he wrote U of C's grounds keeper Jimmy Twohig, "We have had a good deal of fun catching small fish out in the bay. We can hire a row boat for twenty-five cents for a whole day and go out and fish. It is no trouble at all to catch a large quantity of sand perch; similar to the perch which are caught in Lake Michigan, only a little larger. We were out a couple of hours yesterday and caught about fifty, and could have caught many more if we had wanted to catch them fast. We often catch two fish on a line with two hooks. Ruth caught two yesterday. Alonzo, Jr. caught a 'jack fish' about sixteen inches long on one hook and a sand perch on another hook at the same time. We had quite a time pulling them in. I had quite a fight with a big sea trout about eighteen inches long. We have caught about twelve different kinds of fish in our little excursions in the bay. Most of the fish down here have strong jaws and good size teeth.

"You would enjoy the weather here, Jimmy. It is like summer in Chicago most of the time; only never such a cold wind off the lake as is there.

"We are all brown as can be; and are enjoying ourselves immensely."

Later, when Alonzo, Jr. was older, the son would drive a motorcycle around the field during football practices while Stagg rode in a sidecar. Other times when the pain kept him from walking, Mr. Stagg would use an electric cart to get around. Finally, the U of C's class of 1918 gave him the gift of an electric-powered automobile to make football practices easier for him.

"In later years," said Dr. Marc Jantzen, "I talked to him about his bad back and what finally cured him after having been to several specialists and meeting with little success. He gave credit to Stella's hot and cold towel applications over a period of time during their summer vacations at their favorite spot at Idaho Falls, Colorado."

Michigan vs. Chicago, November 30, 1905: The last game under the old rules

The 1905 season -- football's last under the "old rules" -- would go down as the University of Chicago's greatest gridiron campaign. The Maroons got off to a blazing start, winning their first seven games by a margin of 180 to 5. The course wasn't all smooth sailing, though, and adversity surfaced when they played Northwestern in the sixth game of that season. Chicago won the game, 32 to 0, but Leo DeTray was stuck in the eye by the finger of one of the Northwestern players. The injury was so severe that DeTray was ordered to never play football again by his physicians.

Chicago continued on an unbeaten course until their season-ending game with Michigan on Thanksgiving Day. Stagg later wrote, "The background of that titanic struggle was that, for the four preceding years, Michigan had been undefeated. She had won 43 games and scored 2326 points, against a total of 40 points scored by her opponents. In 1905, Michigan had run up a total of 495 points in 12 games, while holding her opponents scoreless. Chicago also had a great team. It had played nine games and had won them all, having scored 243 points to its opponents' 5.

"There was tremendous interest in the game and the largest crowd in the history of football in the middle west -- 25,791 paid admissions -- turned out to see it. The total gate receipts -- $38,500, with each school clearing $17,000 after expenses -- seemed like all the money in the world then. The enthusiasm was unbounded.

"The field was in perfect condition, having been protected by many tons of hay. With my approval, after the game it was to be set fire to. We hoped the gigantic blaze would be a bonfire to victory."

Not every Maroon was so focused on the big game, though, and in the days leading up to it, Mr. Stagg learned that Walter Eckersall and a teammate had failed to keep their curfew. "On the Tuesday before that important game," recalled Mr. Stagg, "I called the men together and told Eckersall and Fred Walker that they owed the team an apology for missing curfew by 35 minutes.

"Eckie said, 'I won't apologize,' and Fred said, 'I won't apologize either.'

"I said, 'All right, you've just forfeited your starting positions,' and I sent them down to the far end of the stadium and told them to practice punting to each other.

"We started to practice and the practice was just rotten. It was terribly discouraging. In about a half hour, our right end Mark Catlin, who had worked his way over to them, came to me and told me they were ready to apologize. They both made a nice apology, so I gave them back their starting positions and the tempo of the practice pepped right up."

The tension surrounding the big game was heightened by hard feelings between Mr. Stagg and Fielding Yost with roots in the 1904 Olympics. That was when Chicago track athlete James Lightbody was approached by James Baird, Michigan's graduate manager of athletics, and offered free tuition and room and board (which was illegal then) if Lightbody left The Midway and transferred to the Ann Arbor school. When Lightbody refused Baird's overture, Yost stepped in and upped the ante by offering the sprinter an allowance of three dollars a week (also illegal). Lightbody still refused, telling Yost, "I don't believe in that kind of athletics."

"The following spring," recalled Mr. Stagg, "I was coaching the track team at a dual meet in Ann Arbor. The schedule of events was firm and had been set at the same time the contract was drawn up. The schedule permitted us using James Lighbody for the quarter and half mile.

"After we arrived in Ann Arbor, however, Michigan's track coach changed the order of events to get back at Lightbody and made it so that he could only compete in one event. I had the contract with me and, after I insisted on the agreed upon order of events being maintained, the Michigan coach and I got into a heated argument.

"Next thing you know, Fielding Yost stepped in and completely lost his head, shouting, 'Stagg, I'm going to stick it to you next fall, and then I'm gonna turn it!'

"I realized that I was on Yost's home ground and that it was no time to carry that argument any further, so I said, 'That's all right, Yost. You've been doing it now for four years, and I expect you'll do it again. You have a wonderful team. We expect to be beaten.'

"Just before that huge game with Michigan, I told the boys about the incident for the first time. Then I said to them, 'I wasn't able to talk to Mr. Yost this past spring as I would have liked to have talked. I expect you to do the talking for me today.'"

Then, the opening kickoff finally arrived, when all issues would be settled on the field. "From the start of the game," wrote Mr. Stagg, "it was shown that the teams were evenly matched. Only once did each team penetrate into the other's territory in the first half. In the whole game, Michigan crossed the midfield stripe one time. Chicago did it nine times. Michigan had a giant line and heavier backs, but the Chicago line held up. The defense of both teams was deadly, and the defenses were so strong that it looked as though a lucky break or a bad mistake would be the only chance of producing a score."

Meanwhile, Leo DeTray had been refused permission by his coach to even step onto the field because of the doctors' orders. Just before the game, though, he begged Stagg again to at least allow him to sit on the bench, and Stagg finally permitted him to do so. De Tray, clad in street clothes, sat wrapped in a big maroon blanket.

When Eckersall punted, and then was walloped by Michigan lineman John Curtis, it was an early indication of what sort of afternoon it was going to be. Curtis wasn't satisfied with knocking the daylights out of the diminutive quarterback, though. He was so intent on taking Eckersall out of the game that he picked up "Little Eckie" and hurled him into the air. Eckersall crashed to the ground a couple of feet away. It was a foolish mistake, because, rather than force the U of C's best player out, Curtis was ejected for his unsportsmanlike conduct. This completely humiliated the Wolverine, since, back in those days, any "Man of Meesheegan" who failed to play the full sixty minutes disgraced Yost, his teammates and even his town.

For several minutes, it appeared that Eckersall wouldn't regain consciousness. Finally, though still dazed, he was able to get to his feet. As usual during those extremely rugged football times, Eckersall wouldn't even consider coming out of the contest, and the game went on.

The first half ended without a score. At halftime, DeTray secretly put on a football uniform and returned to the field wrapped in the blanket. Stagg had no idea that DeTray was on the field, or what the player intended.

"The course of the game began to change in the second half," wrote Stagg, "when Chicago gained possession of the ball in Michigan's territory six times. Once, Chicago reached Michigan's 32-yard line, but the drive stalled, and on another occasion, Eckersall, who had kicked five field goals against Illinois in the preceding game, elected to try a drop kick for a field goal from Michigan's 37-yard line. It failed because it was partially blocked.

"Early in the second half, Michigan got off a tremendous punt which Eckersall fielded on Chicago's 15-yard line. Chicago, though, was penalized half the distance to their goal line, putting the ball on our 8-yard line. Here Eckersall's clever thinking took Chicago out of immediate danger. Calling for a punt and standing well behind the goal line, and with Michigan's linemen rushing through to block the punt, Eckersall chose to run rather than kick, circled to the right, ran between the goal posts and was run out of bounds at Chicago's 23-yard line.

"This feat heartened Chicago and it was not long before she was again in Michigan's territory. Unfortunately, a score did not result. Michigan came back fighting fiercely. A fake punt resulted in a long gainer to almost midfield, but Michigan lost the ball on a fumble two plays later."

After recovering the Wolverine fumble, Chicago continued to play for field position and Eckersall booted one of the longest punts he'd ever made. He launched his kick from midfield (the 55-yard line) and the ball pinwheeled through the air straight to the goal posts, barely short of sailing over the cross bar. It was caught behind the goal line by Michigan back Denny Clark. "Clark attempted to run the ball out of the end zone by circling wide behind the goal posts," said Stagg, "and he was tackled low by Chicago's right tackle Art Badenoch just after he crossed the goal line and instantly after that right end Mark Catlin tackled Clark high." Despite playing with a broken rib, Catlin was on Clark like a demon and hurled the Michigan player to the ground back behind the goal line for safety. Chicago's right halfback Fred Walker stated, "If Clark had gotten by Badenoch, he might have gone all the way for a touchdown. I was playing defense on that side of the field with a leg so badly banged up I could hardly move, and I couldn't have stopped him."

"The excitement was tremendous," continued Stagg. "That safety proved to be the only score in Chicago's 2 to 0 victory." Fielding Yost showed his displeasure by ordering Clark out of the game. Being pulled from a game was the height of shame for any of Yost's men, and, with Curtis' earlier ejection, Michigan was forced to use 13 players that afternoon, when no more than 11 was ever acceptable to " Coach Hurry Up". Clark sobbed as he went to the sidelines. Then, he sat all alone on the bench. Neither his coach nor his teammates would speak to him.

"Denny Clark was anathematized for days for 'pulling the boner'," wrote Stagg. "Unquestionably, he did pull one. One explanation at the time was that Clark thought he saw a chance for a breakaway run and he took it. Shortly before, he had broken loose for fifteen yards after catching a punt near the goal line. Another one is that for five years Michigan's strategy had been to smash her way down the field, even when they started from near their own goal line. Michigan never bothered to punt until the last down. Up to the Chicago game, they had met little resistance and had been able to wear down her opponents and run up big scores. Another explanation was that Clark was imitating Eckersall who only a few plays previously had pulled off his daring run between the goal posts"

Immediately after the Maroons scored the winning safety, Leo DeTray noticed that Fred Walker's leg was giving out and rushed out on the field, against orders and without permission, reported to the referee and substituted for Walker. DeTray had problems seeing, but figured at least he could run. His nose was broken on the very next play, but he finished the game despite the injury to his eye and the condition of his nose. It was at heavy sacrifice. DeTray never recovered the sight of his eye. Denny Clark's fate was worse. He became distraught over his egregious mistake and never got over it. The people back home in Detroit never let him forget his blunder. It gnawed at him for years and led to depression, then eventually to Clark taking his own life.

With their victory, Chicago won a national championship -- the last under the "old rules" -- but their triumph carried with it a tinge of sadness, because it also marked the point college football ceased being purely amateur play. Mr. Stagg, however, would everlastingly remain an "amateur" coach.

A number of players from that 1905 Chicago Maroon squad went on to become college football coaches. Two are in the Hall of Fame -- Hugo Bezdek and Jesse Harper. Bezdek owns the distinction of having coached in three Rose Bowls with three different teams -- Oregon, Penn State and the Mare Island Marines service football team. Harper coached at Notre Dame from 1913-1917 and his teams won 33 games, lost only 5 and tied one. A remarkable fact about Harper being at Notre Dame is that he was an avowed atheist.

Jess Harper's most famous ND squad was the 1913 team led by Knute Rockne and Gus Dorais that used the forward pass in sensational fashion to defeat Army at West Point, 35-13. It was Harper who installed Stagg's offensive scheme of shifting from the T-Formation into a "Box" (a version of the Balanced-Line Single Wing) at Notre Dame. Rockne then used Stagg's offense to establish himself as the most famous coach of his time.

Chicago's triumph had far-reaching effects. It ended Michigan's reign as "Champions of the West", and also led to Michigan's leaving the Big Ten for several years. Yost's team played only one conference game in

1906, none in 1907, then Michigan withdrew from the Western Conference in 1908 and remained outside the league until 1917. A major factor in Michigan's actions was the fact that Yost had become the most "intersectional-minded" coach of all, and the Wolverines had, year after year, booked several games with eastern and southern schools. At that point in time, the Big Ten was cramping Michigan's style. Stagg didn't oppose Michigan and Yost again until 1918, when the male students were part of the Student Army Training Corps and athletic departments had little control over scheduling. In effect, the Stagg vs. Yost rivalry ended Thanksgiving Day, 1905.

Using the contacts he made while coaching football, Fielding Yost became a very wealthy man by promoting and developing a hydroelectric plant, by serving as a director of a cement company and by being an official of a bank. He always regarded huge Michigan Stadium as his true claim to fame. Yost had spent years coaxing, cajoling and arm twisting to get the arena built. Two years before his death in 1946, when the "Big House" seated 87,000, Yost gazed over the "house" he=d built and said, "The best thing about it is that people pay three dollars for every seat in it."

Football begins to "take to the air"

Nineteen hundred and five also marked the end of the old style "mass play" football. In 1904, there were 19 fatalities in the game of football, and it was worse in 1905 when 32 died. "The game of football had become unusually rough by then," said Dr. Marc Jantzen. "The typical game plan included an effort to eliminate the star player on the opposing team by any means possible. This resulted in excessive injuries, and even fatalities." A ripple effect was that these incidents of intentional incapacitation discouraged football players from displaying their talents, since every good player became a marked man.

"Mr. Stagg sought an audience with Teddy Roosevelt," continued Dr. Jantzen. "Stagg believed that getting the forward pass approved by the eastern-dominated rules committee would inject speed and skill into the sport and clean up a game dominated by mass play and brutality. He had been working at this for years, going back to Springfield College, but had been unsuccessful in his efforts. With the president's weight behind it, though, he could accomplish the goal." This conference was made possible by William Rainey Harper being on the banquet committee of a Citizens of Chicago group hosting a $15-a-plate affair honoring President Roosevelt at Chicago's Auditorium on the evening of October 3, 1902. Harper supplied Stagg with an invitation and arranged the meeting. Roosevelt immediately liked the idea, pledged his support to Stagg and, working in concert, they were able to make the passing game a part of football; but it still took them over three years to persuade the rules makers to accept the idea, so that a decade's worth of Stagg' doodlings could finally be brought to life.

"This resulted in Mr. Stagg taking the leading role in establishing a Football Rules Committee," added Dr. Jantzen. "Stagg's committee absorbed the eastern group and eventually became the forerunner of the NCAA." Mr. Stagg was a part of the National Football Rules Committee from its earliest years, was elected a life member in 1932 and served without interruption for 34 years.

Nineteen hundred and six was the first year Stagg was allowed to use his invention and he spent many hours devising the best possible ways to implement the forward pass. "I invented 64 different forward pass plays for that first season," said Stagg, "covering in principle every possible type of pass. I held them under cover, though, with the idea of springing some of them in our most important game; against the University of Minnesota on November 10th.

"We had handily won all of our previous games, so, even though we had assiduously practiced our forward pass formations, we found that it was not necessary to use them. To our terrible dismay, it rained steadily throughout the Minnesota game. Marshall Field was turned into a marsh and Captain Eckersall didn't try a single forward pass because the ball was so slippery. I have always felt that he made a mistake; that he should have at least tried some passes. Luckily for Minnesota, Bobby Marshall, their colored end, was able to make a phenomenal placekick -- a 52-yard field goal. The ball landed on the cross bar and slid over, thus winning the game, 4 to 2 (field goals at that time counted four points). Our score came on a safety.

"All the surprise formations we had prepared for Minnesota, we sprung on Illinois the following week. Illinois was completely nonplussed and mystified and Chicago scored with the greatest frequency through the use of the forward pass. The University of Chicago defeated Illinois 63 to 0.

"Thus was the forward pass formally introduced to the University of Chicago. Thus also was Illinois made the unhappy recipient of what we all felt confident would have happened, perhaps to a lesser degree, to Minnesota. By an accident of that heavy rain, I have always believed Chicago was deprived of winning a championship in the first year of the forward pass rule. However, Chicago went on to win the championship in 1907 and in 1908 because of our clever forward pass formations and skillful use of the forward pass.

"The schools in the east were slow and overly conservative in getting much use out of the forward pass. They used it entirely as a threat, not an integral part of any offense. It wasn't until Notre Dame trounced Army, 35-13, in 1913, using an offense their coach, Jess Harper, learned while playing for me, that eastern coaches became convinced of the necessity of developing the forward pass."

Nineteen hundred and six was also the year Stagg conducted the first summer coaching classes in track and field and football for the benefit of high school and college coaches. In later years, he would conduct coaching clinics all over the country and in the process, became a mentor for many young coaches. One of those who learned a great deal from Stagg and began a lifelong friendship with the Old Man was Lynn "Pappy" Waldorf; who went on to a legendary career, coaching at Oklahoma State, Kansas State, Northwestern and California. Stagg told Waldorf that the key to the coaching profession was the relationship the coach has with his players. "I love all my players," Stagg said. "Some I had no respect for and some I disliked, but I loved them all the same." Stagg also told Waldorf that he wouldn't be able to judge how well any of his teams really did until 20 years after their last season, when he'd know how they fared in life. Another of Stagg's commandments stuck with Pappy, and he carried it like a torch throughout his life: "Your players are your pupils, with more interest in your subject than any of their other classes. For that reason, you should be the best teacher in the school." Stagg had an even more immediate impact on Lynn Waldorf's career when his recommendation resulted in the Methodist bishop's son being hired as an assistant coach at Kansas in 1928 -- an entree into big time football.

Charlie Sarver, an explosive University of California running back known as the "Bakersfield Bullet" and who played for Waldorf, said of Mr. Stagg, "I met him on several occasions and Pappy Waldorf was just like him. They both had the same special quality. If you were in their presence, even if they didn't even know your name, they still gave you the feeling that they really did know you, and that you were their friend. Both of them were very approachable."

Wally Steffen: A master of football and the law

After Walter Eckersall graduated, Stagg shifted 158-pound Wally Steffen from halfback to Eckersall's spot at quarterback. He performed so well that Walter Camp placed him on the 1907 second team All-American squad; and Steffen was a first team All-American in 1908 when he captained Chicago to an unbeaten season. Stagg said of him, "I have never seen a more clever, resourceful, or quicker ball carrier. He was shifty, an artful dodger and a keen, accurate passer. He was a deadly tackler, and could catch and return punts. He was a good punter and drop-kicker, a smart play maker and an inspiring team leader. Add to this his straight-arm ability and you have a great football player."

Steffen began his varsity career the same year that the forward pass was legalized. His talents were well suited for the more open style of play. In three years, he scored 156 points as he led Chicago to many lopsided victories. Steffen served as Stagg's assistant from 1909-1912; then was the head coach at Carnegie Tech in Pittsburgh from 1914 until 1932, when he was elected a superior court judge in Chicago.

Steffen would serve as a judge early in the week while his assistants prepared the team, then he would join his team in Pittsburgh and coach on the weekend. From 1914 - 1932 (no team in 1918), Steffen earned a respectable record of 88 - 53 - 6. He was the first to coach against the fabled 'Four Horseman' of Notre Dame, in 1922. In 1926, he knocked Notre Dame from the ranks of the unbeaten, upsetting the Irish, 19 - 0.

Mr. Stagg wrote about Steffen, "He made so large a reputation as a player that he was immediately judged to be of financial value. He confided to me that he had an offer of $150 per week to appear daily in a vaudeville show. That amount of money was a big temptation to him, but I advised him strongly against accepting it. I felt that it would cheapen him, and he later said it would have done just that. He was always very happy that he didn't accept that offer.

"He also told me that he had an offer of $500 to play in a football game in St. Louis. When he phoned them to refuse their offer, they raised it to $600, then to $700 and to $800. Then the fellow said, 'What in the blazes do you want?' Wally told the man, 'You could never offer me enough. I have talked your offer over with Mr. Stagg and I have decided that it is inadvisable to accept it. That's all there is to it.'"

In 1907, Stagg produced a team which had as much passing skill as any he ever coached. The Maroons won the Big Ten championship that year and repeated in 1908. Along with Wally Steffen, two of Chicago's greatest all-around athletes were on the squad -- John Schommer and Pat Page. In addition to his football talents, Schommer was an All-American basketball player, as well as a fine first baseman and outfielder. Page starred as a southpaw pitcher and was a sensational guard in basketball, as well an excellent football player. With Schommer and Page at the ends and Wally Steffen at quarterback, the Maroons had an excellent passing attack. Stagg devised pass plays still found in every team's play book. John Schommer later said, "When Stagg added the forward pass to the T Formation, then every known play could be run from it. And the only adequate defense against it was a defense against every known play."

Chicago was 4-1 in 1907, with their only loss inflicted by the Carlisle Institute before a packed house at Marshall Field. Pop Warner's "Indians", a team representing a government school with students from over sixty different tribes, was so talent-laden that Jim Thorpe was listed on their roster, but couldn't break into the starting lineup. Late in that game, one of Carlisle's ends suffered an injury, but refused to come out and allow Thorpe to take his position, as a matter of tribal pride. Wally Steffens suffered through the poorest game of his career, and Carlisle won, 18-4. It was a tainted triumph for Carlisle, though, since the Indians' lone touchdown pass was scored by Albert Exendine, who had lined up in a position that made him ineligible as a receiver and to make matters worse, momentarily ran off the field during his sprint for the end zone.

After Michigan's secession from the Western Conference, Minnesota replaced the Wolverines on Chicago's schedule, and Stagg found a new rival in his old Yale teammate and co-author, Dr. Henry Williams. The first meeting of the old "Elis" produced a 6 to 6 tie, then the Golden Gophers proved to be too many and too powerful for Chicago and won nine of the next 13 games. Minnesota was all that stood in the way of Chicago having one of the greatest runs in the history of Big Ten football, because, from 1905 through 1909, Chicago lost only two games -- both to Minnesota. Still, over a seven-season period from 1902-1908, Chicago's record was 52-6-3. Because of this, they acquired the nickname "Monsters of The Midway".

In a 1909 game against Northwestern, Chicago got a lucky break by recovering a fumble at the goal line for what appeared to be an easy touchdown. As the players lined up for the PAT attempt, though, Stagg motioned the officials over to his sideline and said to them, "Gentlemen, I happen to be on the rules committee and I believe you have erred in giving us that touchdown. Chicago is not entitled to that score, as the impetus that put the ball in the end zone did not come from our team." The touchdown was taken away from the Maroons, but Chicago won anyway, 34-0.

Chicago's band director, Gordon Erickson, immortalized Stagg in 1910 with his composition: "Wave the Flag of Old Chicago".

> Wave the flag of Old Chicago,
> Maroon the color grand.
>
> Ever shall the team be victor

Known throughout the land.

With the Grand Old Man to lead them,
Without a peer they'll stand.
Wave again that dear old banner,
For they're heroes every man.

Also in 1910, Stagg arranged an autumn trip for Chicago's baseball team to Japan and the Philippines to play a series of games with Waseda University. This was the first of five such trips between 1910 and 1930. During that period, Waseda University made five exchange visits to the United States.

In 1912, Chicago became the first Big Ten member to play a schedule of strictly conference games and continued doing so for the following two seasons. The Maroons were unbeaten in 1913 (7-0) and won the Big Ten title. Nineteen thirteen was also the end of Chicago's gridiron brilliance, for that was Stagg's last unbeaten and untied squad. The day was coming when no matter how innovative Stagg's tactics were or how masterful his coaching, he could no longer cope with the flood of manpower bolstering the state supported members of the Big Ten.

The 1913 Maroons were a solid, though not a spectacular team, with an All-American center in Paul DesJardien. Years later, DesJardien recalled, "Mr. Stagg was a stickler for training habits. He would tell us, 'Keep the hot dogs in the stands where they belong. I never ate one in my life.' On road trips, he allowed us $1.00 for each meal and if we charged more to the team bill, he collected the difference. 'I am a stoic and not an epicurean,' he would say. Coach Stagg never smoked and frowned on those who did. All old C-Men quickly stamped out their cigarettes when they saw him coming."

Nineteen thirteen was also the year Bob Zuppke became Illinois' head coach. The former Oak Park (Illinois) High School coach, who once had Ernest Hemingway on his team, posed an immediate challenge for Stagg. In the 20 times they would face each other, Zuppke bested Stagg 13 times and tied another and "Zup's" run of six straight was one of the best ever against the Grand Old Man. Zuppke's blustery personality was quite different from Stagg's, a fact he would bring to his banquet circuit audiences' attention by telling them how, "Stagg never swears at his men because he doesn't have any men. He calls this man, then that man, then another, a jackass. By the end of his practices, there are no men playing -- just jackasses grazing."

In 1914, Marshall Field was enlarged with the addition of a $200,000 grandstand and renamed "Stagg Field", thus according Amos Alonzo Stagg the honor of being the first person to ever coach part of their career in a stadium named for them.

With all the hours he devoted to the game, football was not Stagg's only pursuit. He was president of an English folk dance society and, in 1916, he became the first president of the Olympia Fields Country Club, located in Chicago's south suburbs. Its luxuriant grounds encompassed 625 acres and offered four 18-hole golf courses, plus summer cottages. The club originally had 500 members at a time when the village of Olympia Fields had a population of only 150. This was back in the days when a country club was really a country club, when Chicagoans could ride the Illinois Central Railroad down for a weekend at their club in the country. Russell Rugiero, the current manager of the Olympia Fields Country Club, stated, "Coach Stagg helped bring championship golf to Olympia Fields over 80 years ago. His efforts are still realized here as we prepare to host the 2003 U.S. Open."

In 1929, at the age of 67, Stagg admitted, though, that, "While I have a life membership in the Olympia Fields Country Club, which I helped promote and of which I was president during its first four years, I have found it difficult to get time to play golf, and have not played the game for eight years. I still get a lot of fun and exercise, however, out of playing tennis, which I learned after leaving Yale. My young son Paul and I got into the finals in doubles of the University of Chicago Tennis Tournament last summer, but were beaten in four sets by a couple of young professors who have won the event for the past three years."

Stagg's advice to parents

Over the course of his life, Amos Alonzo Stagg not only abstained from alcohol and tobacco, but waged campaigns against them. He described "King Alcohol" as, "A pirate of commerce, parasite of industry, nostrum of medical practice, nemesis of government and universal menace of person and property." He also battled the danger posed by "Tobacco: The Killer". In addition, Stagg was a stalwart warrior in the camp of the National Womens Christian Temperance Union, based in Evanston, Illinois. It was a time when "muscular Christian" could add a lot of weight to a cause, and the Grand Old Man's efforts contributed to passage of constitutional amendments enacting prohibition and giving women the right to vote. He did this to share his experiences as a coach and an educator with the broadest possible audience, especially parents. It is amazing that what he had to offer over seventy-five years ago still rings true.

Stagg wrote, "All the world is a football game and we are the players in it. Too many children are being reared to stand on the sidelines and watch the game of life, instead of being taught to take an active part in it. Athletics, and football in particular, hold a real philosophy of life. The following 'Allegorical All-American Team' is not at all mythical, for it will win every game it plays:

"At the center position is Work; Dependability is at quarterback; Obedience is the fullback; the halfbacks are Self Control and Self Reliance; the guards are Participation and Cooperation; the tackles are Honesty and Courage and the ends are Perseverance and Confidence.

"Indulgent mothers and fathers, sidetracking their responsibilities in rearing children, fail as coaches because they do not install discipline. Training must start from the crib. The great mistake of modern parents is that they put their children on a pedestal, instead of putting them in the game. Without ever having seen the mother of a candidate for the football squad, I can draw a pretty accurate picture of her from the observations I make of her boy -- either on the field or in the classroom. I can tell whether or not she has laid the foundation for his gridiron career from the way he responds to the good player's necessary qualifications. Unless a boy has been taught to be dependable at home, he cannot be depended upon in the crucial test of a game. Unless he has been taught the necessity for work at home, he cannot be expected to work for his coach. This applies not only to his football, but to his whole game of life. Thus, the modern mother cannot smoke or drink without setting a dire example for her children, just as the coach who smokes and drinks cannot expect to obtain the Spartan discipline needed in the courageous contests for his charges.

"First of all, I believe in the Creator and in the order in the universe. We must have order; otherwise, our own relationships do not get themselves adjusted properly. I believe in a strict beginning, which will need long and constant application. The mistake which many parents make is that they love their offspring so much that they put aside the idea of discipline and ruin them from the very start. We should love our children, of course, and love them all the way through, but we should train them to work. We cannot expect to rear children as lazy and irresponsible boys and girls, then later expect them to turn out to be splendid, energetic and dependable men and women. Only a generation ago, there was so much work to be done in the home that the mother required the help of the children. Thus out of necessity, if not intentionally, she taught them to work and to obey.

"Prosperity and greater leisure for the parents of the middle class, which forms the backbone of our nation, now permits them to bring up their children in the manner of the indulgent wealthy -- without work and often with neglect. The mother, without work for her own hands to do, has turned to pleasure and its pursuit, and in so doing neglects her child. The theory that a child must not be crossed to prevent 'breaking his spirit' is not based on fact. Most great men have come up through discipline. The psychology of bringing up a child without discipline is a false one and I have no respect for it.

"With proper discipline, the child will learn to work. I believe strongly in children having to work. They should have their duties in the home. A generation ago, a boy had chores to keep him busy. He had to cut the kindling, chop wood for the fireplace, carry coal for the stove and carry out the ashes, four operations which have been done away within one swoop with one modern convenience -- the oil or gas burning furnace. The girl had to clean the oil lamps, wash and polish the globes and trim the wicks. Today, her sister has just so much more leisure because of the electric light. That is a societal change which must be taken into account.

"The present age seems disposed to try to get something for nothing. One reason for it is that parents are not requiring their children to make a return for what they get. When children are small, what they give is not commensurate with what is being done for them, but we must everlastingly set before them the thought of paying for what they get. Otherwise, it is inevitable that they should always try to get something for nothing; if not honestly, then some other way.

"Participation in the home life results from sharing its work. Participation by the child in the family affairs is most important and vital, but that participation must be complete, not just that of being the idol of the family, but having to do with the work of the family. If that does not occur, a child does not properly relate themselves to the social order -- whether it be with playmates or in their later life. A graduate of the University of Chicago came to see me once, twenty years after graduation. He had been a superior student in school and had reason to expect to do great things in his later life. In our conversation, he said to me, 'Mr. Stagg, I went away from the university with high hopes of what I was going to do in life. I believe one reason I have not accomplished everything that I could have was because I never participated in games when I was a child. I always stood on the sidelines. I am standing on the sidelines in business today.' That's the penalty of non-participation. The child who takes part in games with their classmates and shares in the work of the home acquires the spirit of cooperation. Nature makes us inherently selfish and it is essential to the child's well being that they develop the right relationships; and so fit into the order of living, first at home, then later in the outside world. Cooperation develops what I regard as one of the most essential qualities of manhood or womanhood -- dependability.

"I have placed Work as the center of my 'Allegorical All-Americans', but the quarterback, who is the field general and, therefore the most important member of the team, is Dependability. The doing of things and participation in things tends strongly toward the development of dependability. Completion of the task or the game must be insisted on by parents, for only by completing what has been started can dependability be developed. The man who is dependable is, of course, one who is persistent.

"Some people believe that brains make the man. Certainly one must have a fair amount of them, but unless a boy has been taught to be dependable at home, he cannot be depended upon in the crucial test of a game. Unless he has been taught the necessity for work at home, he cannot be expected to work for his coach. This applies not only to his football, but to his whole game of life."

"Everyone knows that the home has been shattered," added Mr. Stagg. "World War I started it by changing the boundaries of the countries of Europe. The war also

104

shattered the social structure, and we felt it here in this country. During the war, the girls and women took the men's places in thousands of cases. The mothers got busy, went from the homes and did their part in the great crisis. Then after the war, women gained the right to vote and were further drawn away from the home. There have been thousands of mothers who have been loosening their contact with the home. There are thousands of fathers who have done the same thing.

"There was great wealth after the war. We are still in a period of great wealth and I don't know how many thousands of millionaires have been created since. Besides that, a great many thousands have become wealthy; not millionaires, but wealthy. The whole effect has been to put luxury on a pedestal and to exalt pleasure. This has unbalanced thousands of families.

"I tell you, boys, you are living in a time when you must have some self-control. I tell you, fathers and mothers, you are living in a time when you have got to stick close to your boys and girls. Nobody ought to have a boy or a girl who doesn't feel the responsibility of that blessing. None of us are worthy of such a blessing if we don't feel the responsibility very deeply and see that we bear that responsibility all the way from the child's babyhood up through the time they become grown. When my eldest boy was nine years of age, I said to him one day, 'Alonzo, if you ever get into trouble, I want you to come to me.' I kept on saying it from time to time. One Sunday when he was thirteen years of age, he came to me and said, 'Papa, I'm in trouble.' I asked, 'What is the matter, Alonzo?' He told me, 'I am accused of stealing twenty-five cents from the collection box.' I asked him: 'Did you do it?' He replied, 'No.' I asked him, 'Who accused you of doing it?' He said, 'The secretary-treasurer of the Sunday school.'

"I asked him where that man lived and we went over to see him that very evening. For two hours, I talked to him and told him how we had brought up our boy; how we constantly laid emphasis on honesty and how every single chance we had to illustrate it we brought it before the boy. Whenever my son wanted a little money for a good purpose, I gave it to him. It didn't seem possible to me that my boy would go and steal twenty-five cents out of the collection box when he could get it just for the asking. But I couldn't convince that man, and I went away very displeased.

"When we got outside, I said, 'Alonzo, was there any other boy near that desk?' He said, 'Yes, there was one.' 'And do you think he took the money?' I asked. 'No, I don't,' he replied. 'Where does he live?' I asked. He told me and I said, 'Let's go over and see him.'

"The next morning, we went over. We met him outside his home and I invited him over to Jackson Park, where we sat down. At first, I didn't say a word about the stealing, but then I gradually worked into it, and I hadn't been with that boy ten minutes when he told me who took that money -- he confessed to me and later confessed to the secretary-treasurer of the Sunday school. But I want to tell you, if I had not stayed with that boy of mine, and if I hadn't from the beginning of early childhood told him to come to me if he got into trouble, that boy would have gone out into the world with 'Thief' branded on him."

Stagg's relationships with his players

While always mild-mannered, Stagg was a drill sergeant on the practice field and no coach ever maintained stricter discipline. He gave his stars no more leeway than the lowliest scrub. Jim Reber, an All-American center for Chicago in 1919, found this out the hard way. On the first day of spring practice in 1920, Stagg called the squad together, then stopped in the middle of his talk to ask Reber, "How much do you weigh?"

""Two thirty," answered the player.

"Reber," thundered the coach, "do not consider yourself a member of this team until you get your weight down to 210!" Reber wasn't allowed to practice until he pared down to the required weight.

Yet many of Chicago's players fondly recalled the Sunday evening snacks at Stagg's house on Kenwood Avenue. Stella Stagg would set out a couple of loaves of her special home-baked bread and pitchers of milk, and everyone fell to. It was such intimate gatherings with his players that Stagg loved best about being a coach.

Fritz Crisler recalled, "To make sure players knew when it was curfew time, he donated a set of bells for Mitchell Tower on the condition that the school's Alma Mater be played by the bells every evening at 10:05 P.M. 'When you hear the chimes,' he told his squads, 'I expect you to be in bed.' These bells still ring out each night at the appointed hour."

"Norman Barker, a former player of mine," recalled Mr. Stagg, "told me that he had never understood why I had criticized him so much until one time when he happened to mention it to Mrs. Stagg and she instantly remarked, 'Why, Norman, 'Whom the Lord loveth, he chasteneth.'

"Norman then added that, 'The whole thing opened up to me then. I realized that you were trying to develop me and make me a regular on the team. I have always felt very grateful to Mrs. Stagg for throwing light on something I did not really comprehend.'"

Stagg elaborated on this when he said, "I never lambasted or tongue whipped a fellow who I could see right away didn't have football in him. What is the use of doing that to a fellow whom you see right away doesn't have it? If he is trying his best, tell him kindly that he doesn't have any future in the game. I let them stay on, though, as long as they want if they keep trying. Most realize they haven't any future in the game after a while and drop out themselves, and I make certain, when that happens, that they understand there's no disgrace in that. Why criticize a fellow if he is coming out to practice promptly, is obeying all the rules and seems to be doing his best, but just hasn't got what it takes. I never do."

Mr. Stagg once had the occasion to reminisce with Frank Whiting, a former Chicago left end who later became the head of a multimillion-dollar corporation. Whiting brought up how he would never forget his fumbling against Minnesota, a mistake that cost the Maroons a touchdown and, eventually, the game. "There was no one in Whiting's way and he was headed to the end zone," added Stagg. "For some unknown reason -- possibly he had an eye on the grandstand's reaction to the touchdown he most surely seemed headed for -- when he dropped the ball just as he was going over the goal line and did not score. Minnesota recovered, it seemed to turn the entire game around and we wound up losing, 20-7."

Whiting said, "I felt pretty badly after that game. I made up my mind to make up for it when we met Illinois in the next game, but Mr. Stagg used me at every position in practice except my normal left end position, and never with the first unit. As the week went on, I got very sore and was ready to fight anybody. I became very worried that I was not going to get into that Illinois game.

"The meanest thing was what Mr. Stagg did to me in the dressing room before the game. He would never announce the names of the starters until just before we went out on the field. Well, Mr. Stagg had finished his talk and started calling off the names of starting players. Ordinarily, he would start with left end, but this time he saved it 'til last. When he finally came to left end, he looked around among the players three or four times. Then, he even got down on one knee and looked under the benches. Finally, he stood up and said, 'I'm looking for a left end and I can't seem to find any. I guess I'll have to let you, Frank Whiting, play after all.' I was so keyed up after that I could have chewed nails. Every time I got ahold of an Illinois man that afternoon, I shook his timbers. It taught me a lesson, though, I carried with me throughout my life: Stay focused on your goal and don't let up, for once you let up, you'll never get it back."

A.A. Stagg was a totally uncomplicated person. He lived his life strictly according to what he believed, he told his players only what he knew was right and he stubbornly stuck to what he believed in. He never considered a level of constant access as a plague. He lived practically on campus, near the stadium and the athletic department's offices. He made sure he knew all his players by name, and his door was always open to them; though it was a "Dutch door".

His method of "speaking to the masses" at meetings and practices was through the use of epigrams which he called "Stagg Lines": "Fight the good fight.", "The best defense is to never miss a tackle.", "There is no place for a loafer on a football team." These bromides were simple things, but they added up to a way of living, as well as a way to play football.

"The Old Man could be unmercifully sarcastic when occasion demanded," recalled Fritz Crisler. "He used his sarcasm once to give me my enduring nickname of 'Fritz'. We were trying out a new play and on the first run-through I fumbled. 'Run it again,' said Stagg. I fumbled a second time, then a third. Stagg blew his whistle. He walked over to me. 'What's your name?' he demanded, as though he didn't know it.

"'Crisler, sir,' I replied.

"'Oh, Crisler. Are you related to the great performing artist -- the violinist?'

"'No, sir,' I answered.

"'Crisler,' continued Stagg, 'there's a celebrated violinist whose name sounds like yours, but is spelled differently. His name is Fritz Kreisler -- K-R-E-I-S-L-E-R. He's world renowned because he has certain attributes and knows how to use them. He has genius, brains, skill, coordination. He also has great poise and great hands. You, however, are absolutely his opposite. From now on, I'm going to call you 'Fritz just so you'll remember you're the opposite of this great man ... as well as a jackass.'"

Crisler was from Earlville in downstate Illinois. In high school, he weighed only ninety-two pounds and he and a cripple were the only two of the seventeen male students in his high school who didn't play football. After transferring to nearby Mendota (Illinois) High, he played a little bit of football, but an ambition to become a doctor was the dominant influence of his mid-teen years. He graduated second in his class at Mendota High School and went on to the University of Chicago on an academic scholarship.

Mr. Stagg never actually met Crisler at first, and, truth be told, literally stumbled onto him. In recalling the way it happened, Crisler said, "Wearing my freshman cap, I'd stopped to watch football practice. I didn't see Stagg, who was backpedaling away from a play coming in my direction. He crashed into me and we both sprawled to the ground. As we lay there he snapped, 'I see you're a freshman. Why aren't you out here contributing something?'

"Reporting for practice the next day, I took a real pounding. That evening I turned in my uniform.

"A few days later as I walked across the campus, Stagg rode past me on his bicycle, then turned and came back. 'Weren't you out for football?' he wanted to know. 'What happened?'

"'I quit.'

"He just looked at me. 'I never figured you for a quitter,' he said, and pedaled off.

"Next day, I went out for football again."

Fritz Crisler spent 1918 in the Army, returned to Chicago in 1919 and became a basketball star and an outstanding pitcher, as well as all that he accomplished in football. He even made one of the junkets to Japan for the baseball team.

In 1919, Stagg beat Michigan for the last time and in 1921 fielded a squad that would lose only one game in three years. From a purely physical standpoint, the 1921 Maroons formed one of the strongest squads Stagg ever coached, and Fritz, "the opposite", played an important role.

Crisler was a brilliant student. He had to maintain a 90 average to keep his scholarship and did. He needed 144 grade points for a Phi Beta Kappa; he piled up 146, but got three points knocked off for cutting mandatory chapel services. It was traditional that seniors got freshmen to attend chapel for them. Crisler's freshman let him down and kept him from a Phi Beta Kappa key.

Fritz often recounted the most emotional halftime speech he ever heard Stagg deliver. Chicago was behind at halftime to an opponent they should have been handling easily and had brought it all on themselves with mistakes and listless play. Stagg let his team sit by themselves for several minutes, then finally walked into the dressing room. All he said was, "May God have mercy on you! If you play the game of life as you are playing this game, you will all be dismal failures." Then he walked out, slamming the door behind him. Chicago exploded in the second half and won that game in a walkaway.

Crisler also told of a locker room scene during halftime of the game against Illinois his senior year. "We were odds-on favorites," he said, Abut the field was wet and slippery. Illinois had outplayed us in the first half. Stagg came into the locker room, walked around the room slowly, not saying a word. Finally, he broke the dead silence, 'What's wrong out there? Can anyone tell me?'

"" The field is muddy, Mr. Stagg,' I said. 'Our cleats won't hold.'

"The Old Man raised both hands in supplication, then roared, "Conditions are no worse for you than for Illinois! If Beethoven had used his troubles as an excuse, we'd never have had his music! If there's a father's son among you who thinks he's done his level best, stand up and say so.'

"No one stood. 'I'll leave you with your thoughts,' he snapped.

"Lashed by his words, we went out and won that game."

By the end of 1921, Crisler was so hard up financially that he gave up his medical aspirations and took Stagg's offer to become an assistant coach. He worked for Stagg from 1922-29, then went on to a legendary coaching career at Minnesota, Princeton and Michigan. His biggest contribution to the game was his introduction of "two-platoon" football in 1945. Crisler's innovation was the key element of specialization that has made the game even more of a "scientific sport".

The Maroons try to twist the tail of Princeton's Tiger

From the standpoint of college football becoming a national attraction, 1920 marked the game's most successful season up to that point. By that time, the man on the street had become a football fan, all as a result of widespread scheduling of intersectional games: Harvard making a long trip to play Oregon, Notre Dame playing at Army, little Centre from Kentucky traveling to Harvard and Nebraska's "eastern invasion" of Rutgers and Penn State. When Chicago and Princeton scheduled a two-game, home-and-home series beginning in 1921, it marked the beginning of football's first intersectional series.

Chicago won the 1921 contest in New Jersey, 9 to 0. It was the first time any of the "Big Three" -- Harvard, Yale, Princeton -- ever lost to a team from the "west".

The Maroons promised to be even stronger in 1922 and launched that season with three well-played victories. As their home game with Princeton approached, the Tigers weren't conceded much of a chance, but anything can happen on any given Saturday.

Chicago scored three touchdowns without attempting a single forward pass and led,18-7, going into the final period.   Then, all hell broke loose after Princeton was penalized for throwing an illegal forward pass during a punt return and the ball was moved back to their two-yard line.   Instead of punting the ball away from deep in their end of the field, the Tigers took a crazy risk and completed a pass that advanced the ball out to Princeton's 40-yard line. Princeton was held and punted, giving Chicago the ball on the Maroons' 42-yard line.   However, the U of C's starting center was forced from the game because of an injury.   On the very next play, Chicago's substitute center William Dawson made a bad snap and the ball bounced off Willis Zorn's shoulder into the arms of Princeton's left end Howard "Howdy" Gray.   Gray then raced unhampered 43 yards to score, pulling the Tigers close at Chicago 18, Princeton 14.

The next time they got possession of the ball, Princeton again took to the air and, though the pass was incomplete, a pass interference penalty against Otto Strohmeier took the ball down to Chicago's 15-yard line. What made that penalty so bitter for the Maroons to swallow was that the attempted pass was uncatchable. Princeton converted that opportunity into a touchdown and went into the lead at 21 to 18.

Chicago appeared poised to pull it out in the last two minutes of the game, though, as they stitched together a nine-play drive from their 34-yard line down to Princeton's one-yard stripe. Once in this goal-line situation, however, Mr. Stagg's boys forgot everything he had spent the previous week drumming into their heads. "Lewis McMasters was in at quarterback," recalled Stagg, "and for three years, he had repeatedly heard about the absolute inadvisability of trying to power the ball over the middle with only a yard to the end zone. McMasters, though, persisted in doing just that. Had the right plays been used, there isn't the least doubt that Chicago would have made the touchdown and won the game."

A great deal of what transpired in the closing moments of that game was a direct consequence of the previous winter's football rules committee meetings. Stagg had successfully sponsored legislation to prevent using substitutes to relay information from the bench to the playing field; so he felt there was nothing he personally could do in this crucial moment to change his team's selection of plays. Fritz Crisler, then Stagg's assistant, pleaded with the Old Man to send in Amos Alonzo Stagg, Jr., a substitute quarterback, with a play in which Alonzo, Jr. would throw a pass. "Princeton is massed up to stop the inside run," cried Crisler, "the end zone is wide open. Your son will be the hero of the game!" Stagg just shook his head. "No," he said. "I have to live with my conscience. Let the kids work it out by themselves."

So, Stagg's boys were left on their own and did not make an "A" in the test they had prepared for all week. McMasters forgot all of Stagg's coaching, continued to try pounding it up the middle and Chicago was stopped on Princeton's one-yard line. The Ivy League team won, 21-18. The Maroons suffered further disappointment in the final game of that season when Wisconsin held them to a scoreless tie and they dropped into a second-place finish in the Big Ten. None of this caused Mr. Stagg any anguish, though, because he looked at football games as great learning experiences; even the 1922 Chicago-Princeton game. For years, he used it as a case study when he lectured on generalship.

The menace of early pro football

Nineteen twenty-two was also the year Stagg gave pro football its first headline in a metropolitan newspaper when the January 30th *Chicago Herald and Examiner* ran, "Stagg Says Conference Will Break Professional Football Menace". "Professional football would not have been considered an evil if it had been square and above board," said Mr.Stagg, "but because of the elements of money and gambling which entered the picture, it had not been conducted in an honest way. Men were allowed to play under assumed names, and in this way, the pro game was a temptation to the high school athlete and college man to play professional football while also playing as an amateur for his school."

Stagg, however, realized it was inevitable the professional game would grow and prosper as football became more and more a spectator sport. In fact, twenty-one of his University of Chicago players went pro. The most prominent were "Shorty" DesJardiens, who was player-coach of the Chicago Tigers in 1920, and Dick Stahlman, who played 10 seasons from 1924-1933 for six different teams and was on championship Packers and Bears squads. The Old Man even indirectly subsidized Chicago's south side professional team, when Chris O'Brien's Morgan Athletic Club were given cast off U of C football jerseys to use; jerseys which had been laundered so many times that the maroon had faded to a cardinal-red color. O'Brien's team eventually became the NFL's Chicago Cardinals (The Chicago Cardinals later relocated and became the Arizona Cardinals.).

Mr. Stagg encounters the "Galloping Ghost"

In 1923, Chicago won their first four games before they traveled to Champaign, Illinois to face an unbeaten Illinois team with Red Grange. Mr. Stagg said of the redheaded halfback from Wheaton, Illinois who worked hauling ice for spending money, "He was a very gifted and remarkable player who was dangerous because of his speed, intensity and 'struggling ability' -- meaning his capacity to twist and turn and struggle on after being hit. He was particularly gifted on wide runs; because he controlled his speed intelligently, slowing down or bursting as the necessity indicated. He also used a clever hip motion, and possessed a rugged physique." The 1923

117

Chicago-Illinois match up was the very first game played in Champaign's Memorial Stadium (Illinois didn't hold the stadium's "dedication game" against Michigan until the following season.). Unpaved access roads surrounded the stadium, and heavy rains left inches of thick, gooey mud for miles around the arena.

The night before the contest, Chicago's fullback Harry Thomas was declared
ineligible for having missed an examination. This was a crippling last-minute development, since most of the Maroons' attack had been built around Thomas' line plunging ability. Even with this handicap, the Maroons still put forth a great effort; but Red Grange carried 24 times for 101 yards, as well as scoring the game's only touchdown, and Illinois won, 7 to 0. The loss cost Chicago an outright Big Ten championship. The Maroons, Illinois and Michigan wound up sharing the conference title that season. It would be the only year the Illini won even a share of a Big Ten title during Grange's years with them.

The following autumn, 1924, Red Grange captivated America. On the Sunday afternoon before Bob Zuppke, the "Wheaton Iceman" and the rest of the Illini came to Stagg Field, the Old Man patiently listened to his young assistant Fritz Crisler deliver a lengthy scouting report packed with superlatives about "The Galloping Ghost's" ball carrying ability. Finally, Stagg interrupted and said: "All the times you've seen Grange, have you ever seen him score without the ball? No! Now, Fritz, why don't you tell me about how their line plays on defense."

Stagg had noticed that Illinois' defense hadn't really been tested; that Grange had been putting his team in front,

118

enjoying big leads, and Illinois' opponents were running plays out of desperation. He also believed that Zuppke's aggressive linemen would be susceptible to Chicago's cross blocking schemes. He knew this would work because Zuppke had been using small guards, sacrificing size to give Grange downfield blocking help. The more successful Chicago would be at running the ball, the more time they would eat off the clock, and the less opportunities Grange would have.

"It was the biggest game ever played in our stadium," recalled Stagg. "Illinois held off in dedicating their new stadium until they played Michigan in October 1924, and Grange personally took charge of the ceremonies. In twelve minutes, he scored four touchdowns against a mighty Michigan machine, the most spectacular singlehanded performance ever made in a major game. On successive Saturdays, Illinois smashed Michigan, 39-14, and Iowa, 36-0. Up to the Chicago game, Grange had carried the ball seventy-six times for 795 yards, an average of more than ten yards per carry. This was the prospect that faced a presumably ordinary Chicago eleven.

"More than 65,000 had attended the Michigan-Illinois game in Urbana, a town of 12,000, more than 100 miles from the nearest big city. Our capacity at Chicago was only 32,000, and Illinois would have been happy to have all those seats to themselves. Their section in the stands wore a festive, picnic air. As gay parties of congressmen and their ladies jogged out from Washington to grace the First Battle of Bull Run and applaud a Rebel rout, so came Illinois to Stagg Field. In the face of the Iowa and Michigan games, no one asked who would win. The barbecue pits were dug, the fires were banked and it was no secret who was going to provide the meat. The dopesters were concerned only with whether Illinois would equal the 49 to 0 smearing Minnesota had applied on us in 1916, or set a new record in Chicago humiliation.

"Our own stands whistled with a graveyard valor in expectancy of a galloping ghost popping out from behind the first tombstone, and held grimly to their Maroon balloons, which carried the tidings of a Chicago touchdown aloft at big games. I never had doubted that we had a chance, and I had the team believing in itself. Our oldest rooter, Mrs. Stagg's mother, who was eighty-nine and sat just beneath the press box, had no doubts. Mrs. Stagg herself, who sat in the press box and made a chart of each game for me, believed. I couldn't speak, however, for more than these.

"There was one fly in the ointment -- Austin McCarty. He was not standing up under the praise he had received and I was not certain of him. I knew he would perform well on offense, but he was not there as he should have been on defense.

"My fears were well founded, for on Wednesday, he was absent for the traditional alumni banquet without my permission and I had to apologize for his not being there. The next day, I used other fellows in his place at practice and McCarty realized that I meant business.

"Finally on Friday night, he came over to my house and we had a real talk. He cried for twenty minutes and begged me to give him another chance. He kept saying, 'Let me in, Mr. Stagg, I'll show you.' He kept saying that with tears running down his face.

"When I was satisfied that his heart was right, I grasped his hand and said, 'Mac, I'm going to let you in.'"

On the U of C's first offensive snap the following afternoon, Austin McCarty carried inside his right tackle for 15 yards, and it took Red Grange himself to haul him down. McCarty carried the ball each time on a 12-play, 71-yard march (over five yards per carry, earning him the nickname "Five Yards" McCarty). The Maroons' hopes were quickly snuffed on the last of those dozen offensive snaps, though, when McCarty fumbled at the Illini one-yard line. Mr. Stagg later recalled, "McCarty was as keen as a Kentucky thoroughbred. He was so keyed up that he was literally prancing. I think he was just a little too quick on the trigger."

With the ball at their own 10-yard line, Zuppke's men chose to play it safe and punt on first down from their own ten. Earl Britton's kick only went 30 yards, though, to his own 40 and it was returned by William Abbott down to Illinois' 29-yard line. A shorter Chicago drive ensued of 29 yards in nine plays. McCarty scored a touchdown from a yard out, and Chicago enjoyed the first lead at 7-0.

As was the coaching custom then, Illinois elected to kick off after surrendering a touchdown, hoping for a Maroon mistake in fielding the ball, and Chicago mounted another drive from their twenty-yard line after a touchback. It continued for 13 plays and 77 yards until Graham Kernwein got the nose of the ball to almost touch the goal line as the first quarter ended. At the end of the first period, Chicago had produced 12 first downs by 35 plays, all runs, for 218 rushing yards; while Illinois had only one snap, which was a punt.

Harry Thomas scored from a yard out on the first play of the second quarter and Chicago led, 14-0; then Illinois began their first real possession of the game on their 25-yard line. Eleven plays later, Grange raced to his left, then made a diagonal cut clear across the field to score from four yards out, which cut the lead to 14-7. Then, Chicago elected to kick off after Grange's score, and Illinois began again at their ten-yard line. After four plays and a first down, though, Chicago forced Illinois to punt and regained possession of the ball on their 33-yard line.

The Maroons covered 67 yards in only eight plays, all on the ground, and scored a touchdown to go up, 21-7. Unfortunately, they left enough time before the half for Illinois to retaliate and Grange capped off an eight-play, 74-yard drive with his second touchdown to make the score Chicago 21, Illinois 14 at the intermission.

Illinois' initial possession of the second half consisted of only two Grange runs and an attempted pass by The Galloping Ghost; then the Illini were forced to surrender the ball. Three running plays by Chicago didn't add up to a first down, though, and the Maroons punted for the first time. Four plays and a first down later, Illinois' Earl Britton attempted a 53-yard field goal that was wide of its mark.

Chicago took over, but had to punt after just two plays. While trying to field Kernwein's kick, Red Grange was nailed by Harry Thomas and Phil Barto, fumbled the ball, but recovered at his own 20-yard line. On the very next snap, Grange shot around left end, flew down the sideline, cut toward the middle, then went all the way -- 80 yards -- for his third touchdown of the afternoon, which tied the game up at 21-21.

After Earl Britton's ensuing kickoff, the Maroons began at their 20-yard line. Three runs only amounted to eight yards, so Graham Kernwein punted on fourth down. Red Grange was badly jarred while returning the punt five yards to his 47-yard line and Illinois called time out so that Red could be revived and continue in the game.

Getting clobbered didn't seem to affect the Wheaton Iceman; for he picked up 17 yards on his next three carries; then he connected with Chuck Kassel on a long pass that took the ball down to Chicago's 17-yard line. Illinois' drive ran out of steam, though, and Earl Britton tried another field goal; this time a 25-yard attempt that was short. The game remained tied.

Chicago then mounted an eleven-play, 52-yard drive which extended into the fourth quarter and reached Illinois' 28-yard line. All eleven plays had been rushing attempts, then, on third and eight from the 28, 135-pound quarterback Bob Curley threw a pass, but it was broken up by Illinois' Heinie Schultz. On fourth down, Curley attempted a 38-yard drop kick for three points. The kick was short, however, and the ball was grabbed by Ray Gallivan at his 10-yard line and he returned to Illinois' 14. On the next play, Red Grange swung around right end for 33 yards; but that drive became just another Illinois march that fizzled out and they had to resort to Earl Britton attempting a 60-yard field goal. The kick was short by 10 yards and the game remained deadlocked.

Illinois limited the Maroons another three plays, forced them to punt and took over at their 37-yard line. It only took four snaps for the Illini to advance to Chicago's 48. Grange got the call, started to run, decided to throw instead and was intercepted at the Maroon's 35-yard line. The Wheaton Iceman, who had shouldered the hopes of the

123

Orange and Blue, collapsed at midfield after that play, but stubbornly refused to come out of the contest.

He had played every second of what he would later say was "the toughest game I was ever in" and had done more than anyone thought humanly possible, even to the point of complete collapse. When Illinois got the ball back, though, somehow the sorrel-haired jet found enough left in his tank to take off around left end for 51 yards before being angled out of bounds by Bob Curley at Chicago's 39-yard line. There was time left for maybe a handful of plays; but, with Red Grange running the ball, that was time enough for anything to happen.

The action came to a sudden halt, however, for that last burst by Grange wouldn't count after all. Illinois' Ray Gallivan had been cited for holding and the ball was walked all the way back to the Illini one-yard line. There was only one minute left to play.

Ninety-nine yards from victory, Illinois had little choice but to "air it out". After three passes by Earl Britton, however, Illinois had advanced no farther than their 16-yard line, so the decision was made to punt and preserve the tie. Britton's boot was returned ten yards to Illinois' 46 by Bob Curley as the final gun sounded. The "orgy of brawn" ended no sweeter than a sister's kiss, tied at 21 apiece.

In rushing the ball 71 times for 322 yards, Chicago had succeeded in keeping the ball away from Red Grange as much as humanly possible. Illinois, on the other hand, had only 33 rushing plays for 241 yards. Grange, himself, had 24 carries for 207 yards and 3 TD's. Red also caught 2 passes for 41 yards, completed three passes for another 53 yards and returned two punts for 10 yards: A total of 311 yards amassed by the Wheaton Iceman in the toughest game he had ever played. The Grand Old Man always referred to that November struggle as "the Homeric Illinois-Chicago game of 1924".

The week following this sensational game, Minnesota stopped Illinois, 20 to 7, after Grange left the game because of an injury. On the same afternoon, Chicago defeated Northwestern, 3 to 0 to maintain their lead in the conference standings. Chicago's final game of the '24 season against Wisconsin ended in a scoreless tie, but Chicago still won the 1924 Big Ten crown with a conference mark of 3-0-3. It would prove to be their last conference title.

From the standpoint of athletic facilities; nineteen twenty-five was a big year for the Maroons, for Stagg Field's seating capacity was increased to 58,000 in 1925, but it was a tough season for the Maroons on the field. They finished 3-4-1 and their toughest challenge was their third meeting with Red Grange. Even though they held Illinois to only 77 yards in total offense (Grange carried 17 times for minus 8 yards), they lost,13-6.

After Red Grange had played his last game for the University of Illinois, the men who ran pro football jumped at the chance of cashing in on the Wheaton Iceman's enormous popularity and Mr. Stagg became concerned about, "the constant bidding for college players at large sums of money, which caused many players not to finish their college work. With less than a year of college work to do, Red Grange gave up college because of large sums of money and the pressure put on him by men connected with professional football.

"The men who played for me that went into professional baseball or football all told me about it ahead of time and, in every case, stated that it was simply a temporary means of assisting in paying off debts they had incurred. My only argument always was that it was a mistake for a young man not to settle right down searching for the job which was going to be his life's work.

"Furthermore, I believe that earning large sums of money with comparatively little exertion is likely to damage a young man's future a great deal, because he is sure to have larger expectations than the eventual rewards produce and, in many cases, there is a tendency for such a young man to become a 'sporting loafer'. It has been proven that our 'C' men who buckled right down to business of their professions got along fast and were making comparatively large sums of money in a few years; while boys who had stuck by professional sports for several years were not earning anywhere near such salaries."

Mr. Stagg investigates pro football

In December 1925, while "Red Grange's Bears" dominated the sports pages, Mr. Stagg, together with Ohio State athletic director Lynn St. John, met with pro football referee J. R. Holway to gain a true financial picture of the professional game and the overall impact it would have on college football. Holway indicated that, "The Bears are the only team that has made money. Very few people consistently attended professional games because, compared to what they see in college football, the pro game is flat.

"In college football, a man has played perhaps four years in high school. All through the years, he has kept himself physically fit by exercise and participation in other sports. In the summer, he keeps himself in trim by swimming, or some other outdoor work. Play is the height of his ambition. He has no responsibilities to worry him and he plays the game for all he is worth. The professional player, on the other hand, has finished college. He has probably had eight years of football. As soon as he enters the pro game, he usually gets married. He does not want to get hurt because he has responsibilities. He saves himself as much as he can. He cannot keep physically fit because he has to work eight hours a day at a regular job in the off-season; for pro football is actually part-time work. As a result, he does not keep up his physical condition. He plays the game for money and gives as little as he can.

"Professional football is a defensive game; since the players come from different coaches who have different styles of play and they cannot easily adjust to different types of offenses. That is why Grange could not make any big plays in his first pro game. In my opinion, he cannot compare with Jim Thorpe as a football player who can run, block and punt." Mr. Stagg interjected at this point and stated, "Grange is a very fine player who has been overrated in the publicity."

Stagg asked Holway, "It is my understanding that Grange received one third of the gate receipts over the first $14,000 for his first game against the Cardinals. Forty thousand tickets were sold and Grange made around $10,000 for playing in that game. Is that true?"

Holway answered, "Yes it is. The Cardinals lost considerable money in 1924, and this year, prior to the game with Grange, were $5000 or $6000 in the hole. That Thanksgiving game bailed them out. Without Grange as an attraction, though, I don't believe there is any real money in professional football."

Holway further added, "Joe Carr, the president of the National Football League, is not on the inside in any way with the Columbus, Ohio team. He is actually on the staff of the *Ohio State Journal*. He is very sick now with peritonitis. Carr is an honest-leaguer and is doing all he can to make the professional game go and to make it clean by living up to rules, contracts and agreements. He is with the wrong crowd, though. I thought that Carr would try to stop Grange from playing with the Bears this fall, since there is a rule in professional football that a man cannot be approached while he is in college. But Grange was signed and has played."

Stagg was given additional information about the true state of pro football by Warren Brown, sports editor of the Hearst-owned *Chicago Herald-Examiner*. Brown was the first sports scribe to give a great deal of praise to Red Grange. He had taken a special interest in the Wheaton Iceman and, with the full support of both the University of Illinois' president and athletic director, even offered Grange a $31,000-a year position with his paper (including a $5,000 sign-on bonus and $10,000 in advance salary before he would have to start work), provided he finish his last year of college work and graduate. Warren Brown indicated that Hearst was willing to do this because, "They were buying Grange's name. Grange was a 'freak' in football, and the outstanding football player of the age. The name 'Red Grange' was snappy and appealed to the public. If his name had been 'Schnauerbach', he wouldn't have had the opportunities." Thus, despite all the publicity Red Grange generated, it was Grange, not pro football, selling tickets. The pro game would not gain national prominence until it cleaned up its act and showed stability.

Nearly twenty-five years later after pro football had developed and prospered, Mr. Stagg summarized its growth and development when he said, "Professional football got a big push during the depression years when it was hard even for college graduates to get jobs. It became entrenched in the big cities. First, because monied men could be secured in those places to back it financially. Second, because the games are played on Sunday and are not in direct competition with college games. Third, the sports departments of the big metropolitan newspapers were giving it a good deal of support and publicity. Fourth, they were able to build up a sizeable clientele of people in big cities who ordinarily cannot attend Saturday games. Fifth, and most important, the leaders of professional football finally became wise enough not to interfere with intercollegiate sport."

Mr. Stagg is confronted by an athletic program with an illicit recruiting system

When Northwestern University hosted Stagg's Maroons for Dyche Stadium's (now known as Ryan Field) dedication game in November 1926, it turned out to be a whole new experience for the Grand Old Man. He wrote, "The field was muddy because Northwestern did not put a sufficient depth of straw down on it to absorb the moisture. Northwestern received the opening kickoff and their Vic Gustafson, aided by excellent cross blocking, ran straight down the middle of the field without a hand being laid on him and scored a touchdown. That had never happened to the University of Chicago before. The play seemed to stun our team mentally and make them timid.

"Chicago committed several errors which enabled Northwestern to score with great rapidity, so that at the end of the first quarter they had a 24 to 0 lead and were on our five-yard line. Less than a minute later, they had another touchdown. In other words, after sixteen minutes of play, Chicago faced a deficit of 31 points. Nothing comparable to that first quarter had ever occurred in all of Chicago football history. The shock of surrendering that first score off the opening kickoff seemed to have unnerved the entire team. After we gave up the third touchdown, I was at the point of bursting into laughter, but I managed to restrain myself.

"We spent halftime in a miserable unfinished room. I said very little because our showing was just too humiliating for words. The boys showed that they understood their situation, though. They went out for the second half and put up a good battle, although they lost, 38-7.

"It was the first time Northwestern had won a game from Chicago in over ten years. As is my custom, I went into the Northwestern headquarters and congratulated their Coach Thistlethwaite. I regret to say, however, that the Northwestern victory didn't carry my full commendation. I believe I have the Christian spirit and sportsmanship to congratulate a coach for victories year after year if they are won in fair competition. For at least two years, though, Northwestern had an illicit recruiting system which induced many superior athletes to go there. I was informed by a reliable source that the star backfield of Moon Baker, Tiny Lewis and Vic Gustafson were induced by unfair recruiting methods. It is not necessary to cheat or buy players to produce a team of which a school may be proud."

Mr. Stagg believed it was best to handle that situation internally. The course he chose was to stop scheduling Northwestern, a decision which cost both schools a great deal of money in gate receipts. As a result, Chicago no longer played Northwestern after the 1926 game. NU's recruiting irregularities were not cleaned up until Bishop Ernest Lynn Waldorf became a member of the school's board of trustees. He enlisted A.A.'s help in arranging for Northwestern athletic director Tug Wilson to sit at the same table with the clergyman at a luncheon honoring Stagg in March 1933. Bishop Waldorf's meeting Wilson led to the bishop's son -- Lynn "Pappy" Waldorf -- becoming Northwestern's head football coach in 1935.

Necessity is the mother of invention

From 1925 to 1932, the university's interest in not only football, but the entire concept of intercollegiate athletics dwindled. As a result, Chicago's material gradually dried up and their football team's records sunk to only 25-40-4 during those eight seasons. Still, Mr. Stagg saw to it that the athletic department more than carried its own weight. "By being a shrewd schedule maker," said Amos Alonzo, Jr., "my Dad made the University of Chicago over one million dollars in the decade after World War I, over and above operating expenses. For many years, the amount he saved through his frugal administration more than equaled the athletic department's actual expenses." None of this, unfortunately, seemed to matter to the university's hierarchy as the 1930's approached.

"I was forced into doing something different," recalled the Grand Old Man, "when the trustees, because of two undergraduate deans who desired doing away with the whole undergraduate student body, were considering making the university completely a graduate school. They raised the standard for incoming undergraduates, so that the admission's department would no longer accept athletes who carried an 80 percent average in high school. In addition to making it hard to get into the university, they also raised the tuition and, together with the stories going around about Chicago becoming a graduate school, we began to fall behind the other Big Ten teams. So, I turned to the passing game I had begun to develop in 1906.

"I developed an idea in spring practice in 1927 which became a key element in the modern passing offense. It was the principle of a back going in motion for several yards back from the line of scrimmage, then way outside. This back could then receive a deep pass or a flat pass; or serve as a decoy for a pass to an end or a quick pass to another back; or stop to become an additional flanker. One of my halfbacks, Hugh Mendenhall, exclaimed the first time he saw it work, 'Whooee! Look at that 'pea-dinger' go!' So, I called it the 'Pedinger', a name the boys could easily remember -- simple, but effective. Later, the Chicago Bears 'appropriated' this maneuver into their system. I didn't find out about that until one Monday when several of the boys reported to me that, 'Our Pedinger plays were used by the Bears in their game yesterday,' and they wondered if George Halas had been coming to see me."

Halas never consulted with Stagg, figuring that just having the diagrams of the plays were all he really needed.

"Papa Bear" was always a tough man when it came to handing out compliments.

Stagg's Maroons had a mediocre 4-4 season in 1927, but celebrated center Ken Rouse's winning the *Chicago Tribune's* "Silver Football Award", emblematic of being the most valuable player in the Big Ten. Rouse was the first interior lineman to ever win that award.

Dealing with a more modern athlete

By the late 1920's, the game had changed, but young men would always be young men. "One of the things a coach should do when he first meets his squad is to gain their confidence and establishes himself with them," said Stagg. "It is important that he approach certain subjects in the right way and get their good will. Of course, if you have a group you have been handling for a long time, you have already established good will; but, as a rule, you do not have the same boys you had the previous year and they do not know you except by reputation.

"I think it is important you say to the boys right at the start that you have no personal feeling toward any of them. You are their friend and when you make comments, you don't intend to single them out because of any antipathy which you may have toward them and that your criticisms are directed at them for the purpose in improving them in their work and, in that way, improving the team's prospects.

"It is only human for young boys and even mature men to get the idea that you have it in for them when you make some ordinary comment about their work; and they immediately get the reaction that the coach is against them and he isn't going to give them a square deal. You don't want that to happen, for it is hard enough to coach without coaching against one person or more who are fighting with you. What you want to do is to develop to the best possible degree the material you have. If you succeed in getting each candidate who has a fair chance to come up reasonably near to his possibilities, then you are a real coach. Just as a teacher can draw out a particular individual and get them to work to their utmost, a coach has to lead his men and develop them to the best possible degree.

"I think it is wise not only to talk to them about your attitude toward them, but also their attitude toward their work and making the team. I don't think anybody is any good to a team who does not show courage, distinct courage. If a fellow shows right at once that he is afraid, I would have to take into account whether that boy has ever played football or not and then have a chat with him if he had not. If he had played football, then I would sting him privately at first, and if that didn't work, I would possibly sting him publicly. You cannot have men out who 'show the yellow'. It won't pay. They are a drawback to the squad and you cannot stand for it. The boy who cannot take the bumps as they come is not wanted in any football family.

"Certain types of boys get an absolutely erroneous idea as to how essential they are to the team, and they lay down on you under tough conditions. Therefore, the coach has to be mighty wise not to compromise himself or his position. I have seen a number of coaches go on the rocks by toadying up to certain players they think are key men. Far better to tell that player, 'If you won't live up to the rules, what can we tell the other boys?' Be sure to tell this to them, though, without anger, but with frankness.

"I have always been unyielding on the matter of training. I never take a fellow back in the season if he breaks training. I take him back the following year if he shows sorrow about the matter, but never in the year of the season it happens."

In the spring of 1928, Stagg wrote to Maroon end Pat Kelly. "This is a letter from a friend. As you read it, you may not think so. Nevertheless, it is true. I shall speak frankly, even though I know it will hurt your feelings.

"Last fall, you played some in the line, but, although bigger and faster than all of your competitors, you were not a first-string player and spent more time on the bench than in playing.

"Perhaps bench warming is the height of your ambition. As far as I can judge, that seems to be the case. During my years of coaching, I have had a few fellows of that sort. If that is the extent of your ambition, I am sorry for you. It is an unworthy one for a robust, quick, fast-running two hundred pound Irish-blooded American.

"Possibly you feel that you can rest on your laurels of last year and bask in the smiles of your lady friends. I warn you that is dangerous for a fellow of your sort. You already are plenty soft and further softening would be your finish athletically. There are some hardy bucks fighting for the job you were after last year and they beat you to it, and right now they are getting ready to battle all out for that place in the lineup.

"Laziness never gets anybody anywhere in football, as in life. Hard work, with attention to details of fundamentals so that one understands his job, when combined with sustained enthusiasm for it, is what enables men to progress and to win laurels.

"A few weeks ago, I received a letter from one of my former players telling me he had lost his job. He had an excellent opening and I hoped that he would come through.

Instead, he lost out. He did not tell me how he came to lose his job, but I know. Both he and you lack tenacity and sustained enthusiasm in what you undertake. You need to fight your inclinations to 'give up' and to conquer them now or you stand a strong chance of being a 'bench warmer' throughout life.

"To avoid that tragedy is why I am writing you. Making yourself a first class football player is only a side issue, except that in the process of fighting for a place on the team, you should develop the qualities that will make you a strong man and a winner in life."

Upon receiving the letter, Kelly went to see the Grand Old Man and said to him, "Mr. Stagg, you don't think much of me as a football player."

Stagg replied, "We have seven ends. I rank you last. Perhaps some of your fraternity mates have told you that you are a good end.

"You're strong, you're just fairly quick; but you have the physique to make good. There's nothing wrong with you, except that you have the wrong opinion of yourself. It certainly doesn't agree with mine. Pat, your father is Irish, isn't he?"

"Yes."

"Your mother is Irish?"

"Yes."

"Isn't it strange that your father and mother are Irish; but you haven't a bit of Irish in you. It is the strangest thing I know. The Irishman does not always have the persistence. He may not stick, but he will go a ways. You haven't got the emotion of an Irishman."

"After that, he shook my hand, then left," Stagg later recalled, "saying, 'Mr. Stagg, I think you will find a different fellow in me.'

"The next three days, I did see a distinct change, but I didn't think it would last. When the season came around, I did not rank him any differently; but to my surprise, the boy did make good at the end of the season. I recommended him for a letter and, then to my surprise, he was elected captain of the team by the boys.

"He made a very good captain, because he got the group together and he contributed toward a fine morale among the boys. He did the things a good captain can do; namely to take a personal interest in each of the fellows, keep their spirits up and keep them enthusiastic."

Years later, the Grand Old Man received a Christmas letter, along with a package, from Anatol Raysson, one of Kelly's teammates. "The package contained my portrait, which he had painted from photographs," wrote Mr. Stagg. "It was an excellent piece of work. I had not known that he possessed artistic talent and, from his letter, I judged that he had not known it himself until he took up art as a hobby.

"Two or three times when he was playing halfback for Chicago, I had been a bit hard on him. Once, I even called him a 'quadruple jackass'. I remember once asking him, 'What's the matter? Are you afraid?' and getting his disdainful reply, 'No, I'm not afraid.' Then, he tore into the next man he tackled with steel trap ferocity.

"I also remember that before the Minnesota game of 1928, when Bronko Nagurski was playing fullback for the Gophers, I planned a special defense to stop Nagurski's battering ram rushes and placed Raysson in the key position at linebacker behind our weak defensive line on Minnesota's strong side. I told him that Bronko was a two hundred and twenty-pound terror who hit like a pile driver and that he would annihilate us if we ever let him get started. My directions were that when Nagurski carried the ball his way, Anatol must rush directly at him and meet him head on at the line of scrimmage with all the intensity he possessed. I told him that his one hundred and sixty-five pounds were in for a lot of punishment. Anatol Raysson's reply was, 'I am not afraid of him. I'll go up and smash him every time.' And he did again and again with unwavering courage until he injured his shoulder and had to be taken from the game. Minnesota won, 33-7, but it was a real battle as long as Raysson was in.

"The glow of his gracious Christmas gift, costing many hours of time and effort, still warms my heart."

Try as Mr. Stagg's boys might, the Maroons' won-loss record from 1928 through 1932 plummeted to a combined 3-20 mark against Big Ten teams. Rumblings of discontent were heard among the "downtown coaches" grumbling, "He has outlived his usefulness," and "The parade has passed him by." Although his teams weren't winning as often as they had before, the Grand Old Man still had the respect of everyone involved with football, especially organizations monitoring irregularities within the college game. After concluding a thorough study of such irregularities in 1929, the Carnegie Foundation's Howard Savage wrote, "Professor Stagg's letters to prospective university athletes, be they 'shopping around' or merely inquiring concerning matriculation, appear to us to be exemplary. His influence upon alumni and undergraduates is apparently the very best. His stand in the Big Ten for athletic righteousness is worthy of our highest praise. Finally, he appears to have imbued his subordinates with much of his same attitude and spirit." The only concern Savage expressed was how difficult it was going to be finding a man to succeed Stagg equally as scrupulous, sincere and honest in carrying out the ideals of college sport.

The birth of the Shotgun Formation

As Chicago's 1929 season wound down to the final game, the Maroons could claim only a road win over Princeton and just one conference victory. They would end the year at home against the University of Washington, a team that only four years before had played in the Rose Bowl. The Huskies came into the Windy City with four men in their starting lineup 6' 4" or better, and their center and team captain, Paul Jessup, was an amazing 6' 7 " tall. No one gave the Maroons much of a chance and the smallest Stagg Field crowd in ten years -- 15,000 -- was in attendance on a cold, rainy late November afternoon. Those who were not present missed a remarkable performance by Ben Wattenberg from Chicago's Maxwell Street neighborhood, as the Maroons unleashed a new offense, known today as the "Shotgun Formation".

"I started working with Wattenberg when he was a freshman," wrote Stagg. "He had a splendid arm and I thought he had a future as a football player. All through his freshman, sophomore and junior years, though, he had not made good.

"At 170 pounds, he was a husky fellow for those days -- compactly built, powerful, with fair speed -- but he did not come through when he carried the ball and he did not come through defensively. He seemed to be a bit timid about coming up and tackling a man; not terribly so, but enough so that I did not pick him out as an A-1 man.

"In practice, he could hit a man with a pass 35 or 40 yards downfield, but in the games, he couldn't make the throw. He seemed to get more of a thrill seeing how far he could throw the ball than in hitting his man. Many times I personally accused him of having motives which were not the finest and reminded him, 'You have forgotten the main reason you are throwing -- to hit the mark. You seem to get a thrill out of how far you can throw the ball, not whether you hit the target.' I tongue lashed him again and again for being stuck on himself.

"In the middle of the summer before his senior year, I wrote to Wattenberg, 'You have been dubbing around ever since you came here. You have every capability for making a great forward passer and every capability for making the team, and yet you have not come through. There isn't anything physically wrong with you which prevents you making good; it is just within yourself.

"'I do not expect you to come through, but I'm writing you to remind you that your senior year will be your one last chance and to tell you that I have a uniform waiting for you.' He did not answer that letter, but he answered it by his performance in the fall."

Ben Wattenberg wore thick-lensed glasses. Since facemasks were not used in those days, he played without his glasses. The sports writers wrote of the Chicago "miracle passer who could hit receivers even though he was near blind", but, according to Stagg, that wasn't the case. "It is true his eyesight was not perfect, but I was satisfied he could see the man to whom he was throwing. Rumor began to surround Wattenberg when he made a remarkable

140

record of hitting the mark." To help his passer, Stagg innovated the "spot pass" -- the passer throwing to a spot where the receiver should be (still used by today's pros and called a "timing route") -- and drilled his squad until the timing was so perfect that passes could almost be completed blindfolded. The Maroons upset Washington, 26-6, and set a new football passing standard, firing 36 times and completing 20 for 301 yards and two touchdowns. Wattenberg was the best rifleman in the Maroons' militia that day, completing 13 passes in 21 attempts for 162 yards and a touchdown. It was a day of firsts: The first time any football team -- college or pro -- had passed for 300 yards or more in a single game and the first time a team had more passing attempts (36) than rushing attempts (22). Mr. Stagg later wrote that, "The game marked a new epoch in football."

Mr. Hutchins' brave new university

Nineteen twenty-nine was also the year 30-year-old Robert Maynard Hutchins became president of the University of Chicago. Hutchins was a tall man with an imposing presence; charm personified, and one who came across as super bright. He also was a high-profile type and was always in the papers. Prior to becoming U of C's president, Hutchins was head of Yale's law school, where he implemented an ostensibly casual approach to higher education. He didn't believe in mentoring students, which he viewed as "wet nursing", nor did he believe in the discipline of dorm regulations, midterm exams or term papers. Hutchins was once quoted as saying, "The three worst words in education are character, personality and facts. Facts are the core of the anti-intellectual curriculum." He believed in giving students lots of responsibility, lots of accountability without anyone directly checking up on them and lots of rope. Some would hang themselves, others would succeed. Perhaps his most telling remark was, "The object of a university is intellectual, not moral."

Hutchins' new system at the U of C called for no elective courses, no midterms, no term papers; with the undergraduates' entire grades for each school year determined by a single six-hour exam for all their courses in June -- an academic version of a "sudden death playoff". Hutchins also espoused the admittance of 15 and 16-year-olds to college, but disdained academic credit systems and grade point averages. Students could conceivably be awarded degrees without enrolling in a single class, as long as they could pass a comprehensive examination proving they had mastered the core curriculum. Obviously, these measures would not help foster a big-time football program.

Under Hutchins' administration, more and more power was gradually taken from Mr. Stagg, until finally T. Nelson Metcalf, an Oberlin man who had previously been the athletic director at Iowa State, replaced the Grand Old Man as U of C's athletic director. Metcalf's primary role, however, was to oversee the University of Chicago abandoning football.

In explaining his reasons for all of this, Hutchins said, "The game simply hampered the university's efforts to become the kind of institution it aspired to be -- a place devoted to education, research and scholarship. Intercollegiate football has little to do with any of these things and an institution that is to do well in them will have to concentrate upon them and rid itself of irrelevancies, no matter how attractive or profitable. Football has no place in the kind of institution Chicago aspires to be.

"Chicago is one of the few endowed universities in the U.S. that did not grow out of a college. It was founded as a university, to engage in advanced study, research and professional training, together with such basic education as was necessary to prepare students for the graduate level. Its enrollment is comparatively small. Forty percent of the undergraduates were women and a very large number of all undergraduates were working their way through.

"The appeal of the university was to those who shared its aims. Students came to study and the alumni, an unusual proportion of whom were teachers and members of the learned professions, agreed that was what they should be doing.

"Other institutions in the midwest were not as free to develop enough programs to serve the needs of all their students. They all had limitations in the form of governmental or denominational control; they had a different kind of alumni, or a different relationship with them; or they were without the financial resources that the University of Chicago commanded. The university, far from feeling a duty to conform to these other institutions, believed that its principal reason for existence was to criticize and improve upon current educational practices.

"The university hoped to prove that 'normal' young Americans could get excited about the life of the mind. To the disintegrated curriculum in this country, which will frustrate anybody's attempts to make sense of it, the university opposed an intelligible program of education, and the students did get excited about it.

"The ancient Athenians were as crazy about sport as modern Americans are. So were the ancient Romans and the Renaissance Italians. So are contemporary Britons and Germans. But we Americans are the only people in human history who ever got sport mixed up with higher education. In some other countries, university athletic teams are unheard of; in others, like England, the teams are there, but their activities are valued chiefly as affording the opportunity for them and their adherents to assemble in open air. We in America are in a different world.

"Maybe it is a better one, but I doubt it. A symptom of the problem is 'athleticism', which I define as corruption which results from mixing commercialism and athletics. But it goes much deeper...we have no clear idea of what a college or university is. We can't understand these institutions, even if we have graduated from one; but we can grasp the figures on the scoreboard."

Actually, President Hutchins wasn't against football. He saw a glowing future for the game, just not at the college level. "The real hope lies in the slow but steady progress of professional football," Hutchins said. "If the colleges and universities had the courage to take the money out of football by admitting all spectators for free, they could have made it a game instead of a business and removed the temptations that the money has made inevitable and irresistible. Professional football is destined to perform this service to higher education. Not enough people will pay enough money to support big-time intercollegiate football in the style to which it has become accustomed, when for the same price they can see real professionals, their minds unconfused by thoughts of education, play the game with true professional polish.

"When professional football has reached this point, we shall be able to disentangle sport and higher education. Students can play (or not play) as they wish; they may attend and applaud if they like. It will be clear that this is relaxation from higher education, not the main purpose of it. Students will come to college to study. Alumni will believe that this is something a normal, red-blooded, young American can properly do. Donors will understand that they are asked to support the institution, not because it has succeeded in attracting a few boys who are huskier and faster than those representing another college; but because when they give it, their money will be spent in improving education and advancing knowledge. The colleges and universities will then be set free to be as good as they know how to be." It was clear that Robert Maynard Hutchins' concept was at odds with William Rainey Harper's, and that Stagg's days were numbered.

In 1932, Stagg was informed of the university's decision to enforce the provision for his retirement at age 70. "I'm too young to quit," was Stagg's answer. "I know too much. I know how too well. When you do know how, have the ability plus the experience of 43 years, as well as pep and vitality; it isn't time to be laid away on the shelf." As proof, he underwent a complete physical examination which revealed he was in the physical condition of a man twenty years younger.

The Old Man asked for another season or two, but Metcalf rejected Stagg's request to continue as football coach. Instead, the university offered to retain him as chairman of a committee on intercollegiate relations and a contact with the alumni. To that offer, Stagg retorted, "I'm not a salesman, I'm a coach."

Word of Hutchins' plans leaked out and Uof C students spontaneously staged a bonfire on campus. A motorcycle policeman tried to disperse the crowd and was pelted with eggs. Stagg was summoned. One observer remarked that it was the first time the Old Man ever was up after midnight. He hurried to the scene in his electric car, called the students a "lot of jackasses" and restored quiet.

On October 13, 1932, President Hutchins formally announced that, in accordance with the university's stated policies, two distinguished faculty members, Dean Shaller Mathews, head of the divinity school, and Amos Alonzo Stagg, were forced to leave because of mandatory retirement. Hutchins' broom had indeed swept out all of Old Chicago. When the news broke, a group of influential Chicagoans came to Mr. Stagg's home imploring him to run for mayor, but the Grand Old Man told them he had no interest in it. He'd had enough of the politics.

William Morgenstern, a graduate of the university and the school's director of public relations, provided insight about Chicago's abandoning football when he wrote, "Until World War I, Chicago was one of the bigger institutions in the country. During that war, Chicago lost three complete teams in the early part of the 1918 season because of enlistments and assigments to officers training camps.

"The post-WW I period saw college enrollments double and triple. It resulted from the war policy of putting eligible high school graduates into the colleges for preliminary training in the Student Army Training Corps because the War Department simply couldn't handle all the available manpower being inducted. So, it decided to use the colleges as a training ground. It proved to be an effective way of 'democratizing' college and breaking down the notion that college was for the chosen few.

146

"After WW I, there were, in addition to returning players from war service and incoming students, a sudden increase of those wanting to go to college. At first, this increase in students carried the Maroon teams through 1924.

"The state schools felt the effects to the greatest degree, because the endowed colleges, such as Chicago, could not attempt to accommodate this tide of students. They couldn't raise money to put up buildings, nor to increase their faculty with the speed of the state universities which could turn to the legislatures and gain increased appropriations to accommodate the high school graduates clamoring for admission. Nor did the endowed universities think they should do so. And many of the new college students couldn't afford the endowed schools' tuition.

"In addition, from 1892 through 1916, Chicago had not only large comparative size, but it got the best available athletes. It drew heavily from metropolitan high schools; notably Oak Park High School and Hyde Park High. These were schools in prosperous well-to-do communities. The boys in them had the leisure time and the physiques to engage in sports and their high schools gave them fine coaching and fine facilities, which many other schools couldn't do. A good many high schools, particularly in rural areas, didn't even have football teams.

"Then, high school football developed with a rush all over the country. All of a sudden there were a hundred good players for every one before World War I. It was also at this time that alumni of many colleges became concerned with the athletic prestige of their institutions and took direct and vigorous steps to encourage good athletes to go to their schools. This is not saying that the alumni bought players, but they certainly organized to direct the choice of prep players. Chicago and the University of Illinois got no such help, which put them at a competitive disadvantage.

"By the early thirties, the University of Chicago had a larger enrollment than it had before World War I and its undergraduate division was bigger in relation to its graduate division than ever before, but it was still a small university, and purposely so. Not only that, about a third of its undergraduates were transfer students who came to get the prestige of a degree from Chicago. They obviously weren't athletes, for athletes weren't going to sacrifice a year of eligibility by going somewhere else.

"The University of Chicago also pointed to the forces of change that were occurring during the thirties; such as reorganization of elementary and secondary schools, the development of junior colleges and the great advance of professional football, which made the character and pursuit of football as it existed at Chicago to be practically impossible. Robert Maynard Hutchins didn't kill Maroon football. Social change did."

Nineteen thirty-nine marked Chicago's final Big Ten football campaign; then there would be no more football at the U of C until 1969, when the board of trustees responded to a petition to bring the game back to The Midway signed by fifteen hundred students in three days. 58,000-seat Stagg Field lay fallow until 1942 when Enrico Fermi and his colleagues used a squash court under its stands to produce the first controlled, self-sustaining nuclear chain reaction and usher in the atomic age. The demolition of Stagg Field commenced in 1957, and the site is now occupied by the Joseph Regenstein Library. Today, there is a new era at the University of Chicago and Robert Maynard Hutchins has to be spinning in his grave. The

Maroons now compete as a member of the University Athletic Association at the NCAA Division III level and will soon enjoy the benefits of a state-of-the-art Gerald Ratner Athletic Complex.

Stagg's leaving Chicago presaged a dramatic change in the city's relationship with the pigskin game, as pro football moved to center stage. The joint efforts of Northwestern University athletic director Tug Wilson and *Chicago Tribune* sports editor Arch Ward resulted in the College All-Star Game; an annual match up of the defending pro "World Champions" against an all-star squad chosen by the nation's football fans. For nearly half a century, it packed Soldier Field and the week leading up to the game produced each year's biggest sports gathering.

Meanwhile, the Bears went on a tear, using the Grand Old Man's offense to chalk up four World Championships in seven years. This encouraged Halas to emulate his friend George Preston Marshall, owner of the Washington Redskins, and hire a songwriter to extol how the Bears "thrilled the nation with their T-Formation." The words should have been, "with Stagg's T-Formation". Halas also publicly boasted of how his organization's innovative offense created a demand for former Bear players as college head coaches. He even profiteered off the Grand Old Man's ideas by publishing a book, "The Modern Formation With Man in Motion" by Ralph Jones, Clark Shaughnessy and George Halas.

After confiscating Stagg's offense, Halas next appropriated the exact University of Chicago design of a "C" for his Bears and even adopted their "Monsters of the Midway" moniker. Next, "Papa Bear" eventually forced the south side Cardinals to leave the city. With the demise of the College All-Star Game, Chicago ceased to be a football city and became a Bears town where football is generally perceived as much more of a business than a game.

Stagg's journey from Chicago to Stockton begins

The last months of 1932 were a time of sorrow on The Midway. There was sadness because of Stagg's parting, and also because of the Maroons dismal season. Chicago was 3-4-1 that season, with only one win coming in Big Ten play. The Maroons' last game that year was against Doc Spears' Wisconsin Badgers at Stagg Field. 20,000 attended the chilly November afternoon's proceedings, which marked the Grand Old Man's final act on The Midway.

In his 41 years with his Maroons, Stagg had had his great players, great teams and champions; but none gave him more satisfaction than his 1932 squad, for none displayed more courage against a stacked deck. They were outweighed and, more often than not, outplayed, but never outfought. It would have been a story book ending if they had brought the Old Man a victory in his last game for the U of C, but such was not to be. Wisconsin won, 18-7, but the score didn't seem all that important. As the scoreboard clock ticked off the last moments of his 41-year career at the University of Chicago, Stagg sat in the midst of his players on a hay-strewn sideline with the just the nicest smile you could imagine on his face. He was with his boys and he truly loved each and every one of them, and no one could ever take that moment from him.

That December, things looked very bleak for the Old Man. In those days before unemployment compensation, social security, "safety nets" or "golden parachutes", a huge anchor of worry weighed on Amos Alonzo Stagg. He had been one of the most acclaimed men in his field, but now he was out of work, with no immediate prospects of employment and eight other people to worry about. If that wasn't enough to bear, a flu epidemic had blown into the Windy City and everyone else in his house was sick in bed. It was enough to drive a man to drink. Trouble was, the Old Man never touched a drop in his life.

Stagg decided that a short walk to his office was what he needed to escape the flu-ridden house. His own health was excellent and he had no problem whatsoever pounding up the stairs to his office on the second floor of the University of Chicago's gymnasium. As he unlocked the door to his office, he thought to himself, "This used to be mine, but will soon be someone else's. Then again, the way things have been going, they may use it for storage."

Stagg spent the afternoon at a typewriter catching up on correspondence. The first letter he answered was from Fred Speik, one of his former All-Americans and assistant coaches who was then a prominent physician in California treating many famous directors and Hollywood stars. Speik mentioned that he had contacted Stanford on Stagg's behalf, suggesting that they waste no time in hiring the Grand Old Man.

"It was awfully nice of you, Fred, to write to the Stanford people," Stagg pecked out on his typewriter. "I don't believe there is one chance in a hundred, though, that they would take me on. First, because they have two young fellows in Tiny Thornhill and Ernie Nevers for whom the alumni are strong. Second, Chicago's record has been so poor of recent years, because of the poor material, that my stock is way down. Third, they would regard me as too old.

"Evidently, Fred, I made a mistake in being too loyal to the University of Chicago. They are turning me out now when I would have a chance to recover some of my prestige. Next year's sophomores promise to be the best we have ever had in all the years of the university. If I had the material they have at Northwestern, Purdue, Michigan and all the other Big Ten universities, I would eat my shirt if I could not do a better job than most of their coaches. It may be immodest in me in saying it, but I know I was never in as good shape to coach football as I am at the present time, and if I could get located where there was some good material, I know I could produce.

"Matters have come to a head, however, and I shall be out of the university. I asked the president for the opportunity to coach for two or three years longer to regain some of the prestige which I have lost during these several lean years. The opportunity was not granted. Finally, I asked for one more season, but that was turned down.

"The university has kindly offered me a $5,000 job which, with my retirement allowance of $3000, would give me my full $8000 salary. It would seem foolish to most people for me not to accept such an opportunity in these days, but, while I have eight people on my hands and need the money, under the circumstances I could not accept it, and I am out.

"Because I have loyally stuck by the university during these lean years, in the early part of which I could have gone to another good university at a salary of $12,000, I have lost so much prestige that I will undoubtedly be relegated to a job in a minor league. For some people, that would be a tragedy, but it will not be completely so for me; for, above all, I am interested in helping young men. However, I do have two regrets. One is that I will not have a chance to regain any prestige by demonstrating that, with prospectively good material for next season, I am still a good coach. The second is that I shall not be able to fulfill the secret desire I have been cherishing for several years: To bequeath to the university the results of my studies and experiments in such permanent form that they might be of considerable future value to my successors."

His world brightened the very next day, though, when he received a telegram from Everett Stark, who was president of the College of the Pacific's San Francisco alumni club, asking if he would be interested in becoming Pacific's athletic director and football coach. Stagg immediately wired back an affirmative answer: Yes, he would be interested and he would like further details of the proposition. Stark's wire had been sent without the knowledge of C.O.P.'s president Tully Knoles, but, as soon as he received Stagg's answer, Starks reached the college president, informed him of what he was up to and wrote Mr. Stagg explaining that, "After reading you desired an active coaching position, our hopes arose that we might interest you in the oldest educational institution on the Pacific coast, yet one of the most progressive.

"You undoubtedly will receive other offers of higher salaries than Pacific will be able to offer you, Mr. Stagg, but you will have to look far to find another institution that maintains the high moral, cultural and scholastic standards that Pacific does and where you will be appreciated more for the fine ideals and sterling character that you are known to possess.

"Founded in 1851 by the Methodist church, the college has educated some of the most prominent men in the state of California. Dr. Tully C. Knoles, the president, is one of the outstanding educators of the Pacific coast and is a fine Christian man with vision, ideals and a capacity for the leadership of youth. He is the kind of man who will fully appreciate the type of work that you do and is one with whom you would find it a pleasure to associate. Should you accept the offer that I am confident that Dr. Knoles will make to you, you will have a splendid opportunity to exercise your individuality and any ideas that you have, unhampered by the administration.

"The College of the Pacific is located on a beautiful new campus three miles from the town of Stockton in the fertile San Joaquin Valley. Furthermore, it is the only institution of its type in the entire Sacramento and San Joaquin Valley area. The campus is modern and progressive in every respect. The average student comes from a good home and is of good intelligence.

"The campus and the college's spirit, I believe, you will find difficult to duplicate in any institution. This spirit and loyalty extends past graduation and you will find enthusiastic alumni clubs in every section of California.

"With Coach 'Pop' Warner leaving Stanford, it seems as if the stage is perfectly set for you to be most favorably received into California sports circles. Aside from your influence as a coach, your published opinions concerning football have been eagerly read by sportsmen of the west, and we would be more than proud to have these originate in California."

Pacific's president Tully Knoles also wired Stagg, then followed with a letter in which he was candid about how small the 450-enrollment college's athletic budget was

154

and asked Mr. Stagg for, "the lowest figure at which you would be willing to come to us, provided other arrangements would be satisfactory." President Knoles added that he hoped that Stagg would be attending the East-West Shrine Game in San Francisco on January 2, 1933, so that the coach could visit C.O.P. and discuss the situation and enclosed a C.O.P. catalogue. Stagg had no plans for attending the game in San Francisco, however, because he was committed to being on the east coast for a Phillips Exeter Academy reunion and the AFCA's annual meetings in New York.

Stagg went through the catalogue the day it arrived in the mail. Shortly after, he wrote Babe Meigs, one of the players on Chicago's 1905 national champions (Babe Meigs went on to publish the *Chicago Herald-American* and demonstrated his commitment as a pioneer in aviation by creating Chicago's Meigs Field airport.): "I do not know where I shall coach next year. Doubtless in some minor league because big league jobs are never open to men of doubtful prestige, and they would shy away from one who is seventy years old. So far, the only one who expresses eagerness to get me is the College of the Pacific, located at Stockton, California. I haven't got full information about it,only a catalogue; but the catalogue does state that: 'In the interest of scholarship, health and morals, the trustees and the faculty forbid the use of intoxicating beverages, gambling and other such practices as are found to be distracting and harmful. Whenever it is obvious that a student is not in accord with the interests and ideals regarded as vital by the administration, his registration may be canceled, even though no specific offense be charged against him.'

"I confess to liking the above statement."

Still, everything Mr. Stagg learned about the school pointed to the fact that C.O.P. was hardly the place to build a big time football program. When Stagg mentioned his possible move to California to friends in the coaching profession, they all wondered why in the world he would ever consider such a move.

Right after Christmas, Stagg went back east to attend the Phillips Exeter reunion and the coaches' convention. Stella, however, stayed home because of the myriad details involved with their relocating; a task made even more difficult because neither of them knew for sure where they bound for. She had gotten over the flu, was feeling peppier; and it was comforting for her to observe how enthusiastically Paul, her youngest, went about culling down his possessions and getting things squared away before he left for graduate school at Columbia University in New York.

Within the previous month, everything had been turned topsy-turvy. Her nest had emptied out and she had no idea where a new roost for Lon and her would be; but she was ready to embark on any course, secure in knowing Lon would be with her all along the way. Then, her world was rocked when a telegram arrived telling her that Lon had taken ill and that he had been admitted into a hospital in New York City.

"Hell's Bells!" was all she could think. "As if there wasn't already enough going on! This could be very serious. After all, Lon was seventy years old."

She had cautioned him about an overcrowded schedule of speeches and not getting enough rest. She suddenly remembered what it was like, years before, when he had pneumonia and hallucinated. At least then she was at his side and was there to take his hand and talk to him; and, even though he couldn't hear all the words, she always believed that the sound of her voice made him strong enough to keep on fighting his way to recovery. But now, none of that could be done from a thousand miles away. She didn't know what to do. "Should I stay and hope to hear something," she thought, "or should I go to him? What should I do, what should I do?" New Year's Eve 1932 became a day of solitary anguish for her; and a long, lonely sleepless night ensued.

With the morning sun, though, a new day dawned and a new year had arrived. Stella received Lon's answer to a telegram she had sent which told her, "Usual influenza. Temperature ranges from one hundred to one hundred one and a half. Have special nurses. Stay home. All my love. Lon"

A weight had been lifted. Whispers of how fleeting life was, though, still rang in Stella's mind, causing Lon"s favorite biblical reference to jump out at her, "That when our time on earth is over, there will be no more planning or anticipation; that we must seize the day." Lon's illness had brought home the fact that her role as a mother raising children was over, but that she still had a life to live and there had to be no regrets when it was all said and done. It was a time for change. She began to make plans and to think about what she would really like to do.

After Stagg arrived home from New York, he received a letter from Tully Knoles, who wrote that, "The College can obligate itself for $3000 of your salary, and the Comptroller and I think that, through outside sources in the city of Stockton, we can secure an additional $2000." With Stagg's $3000 University of Chicago pension, this would mean that his annual income would be the same as it was at the U of C: $8000 per year.

Knoles also indicated he would be in Chicago at the end of that month to meet with Methodist Board of Education and he invited Stagg to get together with him. As a result, Mr. Stagg met with Pacific's president in a Methodist book store's office on January 31, 1933.

Tully Knoles turned out to be a man of action, a marked contrast to U of C's President Hutchins, who once quipped, "Whenever I feel the urge to exercise, I lie down until the urge goes away." Knoles had a great love for football and he mentioned to Stagg that he once rode a bicycle 38 miles to see Stagg's Chicago team play Stanford back in 1894; then seven years later, he was USC's quarterback. Knoles was also a fine horseman, a better than fair hand with a lasso and, with his neatly-trimmed goatee, wearing his cowboy hat and atop a mount, he looked just like Buffalo Bill Cody.

Their meeting didn't take long and Stagg agreed to become Pacific's football coach for a salary of $5000, payable in 12 monthly installments, with the contract to begin October 1st, 1933. He was allowed to hire one full-time assistant coach and he chose to take along his former player Lawrence Apitz, who had assisted him at Chicago. He would also be allowed four paid months of the year to spend however he wished in promoting football. In addition, he was given the deciding voice in scheduling of games, selection of football uniforms and equipment and, reflective of C.O.P.'s tight athletic budget, the number of footballs the team must have. Knoles had a formal memorandum of agreement drawn up on February 7th after his return to the west coast, which he mailed to Stagg for his signature.

After accepting Knoles' offer, Stagg showed the president a letter he had written to William Rainey Harper in 1890 which stated, "After much thought and prayer, I have decided that I best can serve my Master's interest by devoting my life to the training of young men." Stagg said to Dr. Knoles, "In the same spirit, I will come to the College of the Pacific."

When Lon filled Stella in on all that had taken place during his meeting with President Knoles, the only question she had was about the lack of coaching help because of his being able to hire only one assistant. He agreed that things would be rugged with only one man to help him. So, she asked him, "What if you had a man and a woman to work with you?"

Lon asked her what she meant by that. She answered by telling him about the sleepless New Year's Eve she'd spent apart from him when he was in the hospital in New York. Then, she asked him if, since their last chick had left the nest and they would be starting all over again in California, it was all right with him if she did something she had always really wanted to do.

"Of course," said Lon.

"What I really want to do," said Stella, with a gleam in her eye, "is be a football coach and work with you."

Stella got her wish and became an excellent assistant coach for the Grand Old Man at C.O.P. She was well prepared for this, since from the earliest days of football on The Midway, she had sat in the press box and charted each of the Maroon's home games. She became an excellent scout and truly enjoyed breaking down game films. She even taught her oldest son, Alonzo, Jr. how to scout. She was also very good at conducting "chalk talks". Whenever the Grand Old Man was asked if Stella really did any coaching, he would invariably answer: "Actually, she's a much better coach than I am."

In addition, Stella kept tremendous records, not just for the University of Chicago's athletic department, but also for the Big Ten and even the Football Rules Committee. "One time, the Football Rules Committee tried to recreate some of its early minutes which had been lost," recalled Dr. Marc Jantzen. "They asked the Staggs for assistance. Mrs. Stagg, from the files she kept in orange crates and in her kitchen cupboards, had the necessary information. The committee offered to send in a stenographer to help Stella. She would have none of it and reestablished the lost minutes on her own."

So it came to pass that Amos Alonzo Stagg, at an age when many would be seeking a life of ease, agreed to relocate thousands of miles away to a state he'd barely ever set foot in and coach a team he hadn't recruited for a college he'd never seen. His coaching friends figured it had to be because of the weather, but Stagg told them, "California's climate had nothing to do with my decision. Forty years ago, I came west to do some missionary work for Dr. Harper. Now, I'm going farther west to do some more missionary work."

GO WEST, OLD MAN, GO WEST

The Grand Old Man first arrived in Stockton during March 1933; ready to conduct spring football practice, while Stella tied up loose ends back in Chicago and would return with him in the fall. Stockton then was a city of 70,000 nestled in the San Joaquin Valley between San Francisco and the Sierra Nevada Mountains that had been founded during the Gold Rush days as a supply point, but had grown as an inland seaport and rail center for shipping the valley's farm produce. It could easily be described as a "Sinclair Lewis town". He was startled by a huge contingent which met his train and he even became part of a parade, complete with marching bands, that led the way to welcoming ceremonies at the local civic auditorium. It was clear that Amos Alonzo Stagg was the biggest thing to hit Stockton since the discovery of gold, but he could see there was lots of work to do. Outside of California, few people had heard of the place.

"When I arrived," said Stagg, "I was immediately impressed by, first, the college had a poor reputation in football; second, it was not well known; third, the college had a heavy mortgage and, fourth, it was financially in poor shape. It became apparent to me that my special problems were to help make the College of the Pacific become well known and to arrange a schedule of games that would bring good financial returns to the college.

"It was self-evident that in arranging a schedule I had to forget my reputation as a coach and schedule games in which I knew that we would be outclassed and often suffer bad defeats that would mar the personal record that I had already achieved.

"The decision was not hard for me to make, for early in life I had promised God that I would work with young men in His service as long as I could.

"While from a scoreboard point of view the results were not good, financially it worked out well for the college.

"The careful planning and economies of the college paid off. In March 1946, the college held a big dinner during which we celebrated the burning of the mortgage by vice president and comptroller O.H. Ritter.

"During the fourteen years of my coaching, the college netted $229,948.85 from football (equivalent to $5.3 million in today's dollars)."

"In Coach Stagg's first few years at C.O.P.," recalled Jack Cechini, "he proceeded to schedule games with such teams as U.S.C., California and St. Mary's on successive weekends!!! When you consider that in his early years at C.O.P., Coach Stagg had a team comprised of approximately 33 boys, half of whom had played very little football before coming to college; such a schedule brought forth cries of protest from various citizens of the community who personally felt Mr. Stagg was committing 'mass suicide' with his team. I recall vividly Coach Stagg's remarks in the dressing room in 1934 before the U.S.C. game. He softly remarked, 'I look upon the situation in this manner: If you don't schedule the 'Big Fellow' how can you ever expect to defeat him? And I wouldn't have scheduled the games if I didn't have confidence in each of you boys and your ability. I am convinced you boys are capable of winning the game.'

"Well, Pacific didn't defeat any of their major opponents that year. The scores, however, were indicative that Coach Stagg's confidence in his boys was not misplaced -- U.S.C. 6, C.O.P. 0; California 7, C.O.P. 6; St. Mary's 0, C.O.P. 0."

Stagg didn't find much in the way of football talent in the beginning, but what talent there was, he found willing and eager. His first season with the "Tigers" produced a 5-5 record. Highlights were wins over the Cal Aggies (now UC Davis), 13-7; Chico State, 14-0, and Fresno State, 12-0. They suffered heartbreaking losses to San Jose State, 12-6 (when they surrendered a touchdown off of a 60-yard interception return) and to Nevada, 7-0 (when they ended the game on the Wolfpack's one-yard line). The Tigers played their finest game of that season in a 7 to 0 Armistice Day loss to nationally-ranked St. Mary's of Moraga. During that first season, Mr. Stagg demonstrated his commitment to C.O.P.'s solvency when he purchased 21 acres of adjoining land for $3000 and immediately donated it to the college.

"Although Coach Stagg never made it a practice to stress the importance of winning a particular game," added Jack Cechini, "his hold on the boys was so amazing that every time the team took the field they played their hearts out; not for school, girl friend, family, or publicity, but for Mr.Stagg.

"After Pacific's 1935 loss to San Jose State, Bill Ijams, our star right tackle, who had played a tremendous game, came into the dressing room crying like a child. Suddenly, he arose from where he had seated himself and, while smashing his fists against the steel lockers, cried out:

'I let Mr. Stagg down out there!! We all let him down!! In fact, the way we played was an insult to our coach!!'

"Before we could calm Ijams down, he had badly smashed all of the knuckles of his right fist."

Two years later, in 1936, Pacific's already small coaching staff was further reduced when Laurie Apitz left to become head coach at the University of Louisville. Despite this added difficulty, Pacific won the Far Western Conference by going unbeaten and unscored upon in their conference contests: The first time any of Stagg's teams had produced a perfect defensive record. Stella Stagg had shouldered even more of the coaching burden that year and her contributions were recognized by the players when they presented her with a trophy cup inscribed: "Coach of the Year".

With C.O.P.'s constant scraping to remain solvent, President Tully Knoles, in that same year, 1936, spearheaded the move to establish Stockton College on the C.O.P. campus. It was supported by public funds and offered a two-year curriculum embracing the first two years of college work. To avoid duplication, the College of the Pacific limited its curriculum to junior, senior and graduate years. A unique educational situation resulted: A public junior college and a private senior college sharing the same campus, facilities, traditions, privileges and, to a large extent, the same faculty. Pacific thus became the only three-year liberal arts' college in the nation.

"At the close of the 1936 season, just before Pacific's final game with the San Diego Marines in San Diego," recalled Jack Cechini, "five of the first stringers decided to celebrate the end of the season a little ahead of time. Mr.

Stagg learned of the incident and the day before the game, he called the five offenders to his room to discuss the situation. Mr. Stagg pointed out that he did not want to believe what he had heard, but he was going to leave it up to each individual to confirm or deny the charges. When the players admitted their part, he said to them with tears in his eyes, 'I'm terribly sorry this thing had to happen, but you boys know the rules. You have not kept faith with yourselves or with the team. The graduate manager will furnish you with your tickets back to Stockton. You are not playing in tomorrow's game.'

"And so, Pacific played the game the next day without five of its regulars. We proceeded to win anyway."

"Coach Stagg was always ready and willing to assist his boys in any manner possible," added Jack Cechini. "During my last year at C.O.P., after having completed my years of eligibility to play football, I was stricken by an attack of appendicitis. It was near the end of the school term and I didn't want anyone to know of my predicament because: (a) I wanted to graduate and go on to law school and (b) I simply did not have the funds to cover the cost of the operation.

"Somehow Coach Stagg 'sensed' my condition and one day he called at my home to personally discuss the situation with me. Coach Stagg told me I was foolish to 'gamble' with my health and advised me to go to the hospital immediately and have the matter taken care of. Not only that, but he informed me that, if I was financially unable, he would personally see to it that all my expenses were taken care of. By that, Coach Stagg meant that he was willing to personally absorb the costs for my operation, since he realized I was financially unable to do so."

Tiny Pacific takes on the Fighting Irish

During the summer of 1938, Amos Alonzo and Stella were driving cross country and headed back east, when they decided to stop at the University of Notre Dame and tour the campus. Elmer Layden, ND's athletic director and head football coach, upon hearing that the Staggs were on campus, rushed over to greet the Grand Old Man. In the course of their conversation, Layden told him about all the plans involved with the world premiere of the movie "Knute Rockne: All-American" to be held in South Bend during the first weekend of October 1940, including celebration of "National Knute Rockne Week". Stagg appeared in the movie, playing himself in a cameo role, and Because of Stagg's close ties to Rockne and to Notre Dame, Layden proposed that C.O.P. play at ND that weekend as part of that weekend's attractions, and Stagg accepted.

This game would give Pacific tremendous exposure, but it also exposed the school's virtually nonexistent scouting budget. So, not being able to afford any scouting trips to the midwest, the Grand Old Man dipped into his "football espionage fund" -- a cigar box full of three-cent stamps -- and fired off an S.O.S. to the coach at another Methodist school that faced Notre Dame each season: Lynn "Pappy" Waldorf at Northwestern University.

Stagg wrote Waldorf asking if he could borrow NU's game film after Northwestern played ND during the last weekend of the 1939 season. Pappy answered the letter with a long distance phone call and told Stagg, "I'll see to it you'll be sent not only our film, but all of our scouting reports immediately after we play 'em." The Old Man

166

thanked Waldorf, but said, "Just the movie will do. Stella and I like to see things for ourselves."

After the 1939 season, Stagg received a package from Evanston which really loaded up his off season plate. It contained not only a movie of the Northwestern-Notre Dame game, but seven other 1939 Fighting Irish games -- practically the entire season. Stella spent hours charting each game, filling two composition books for every contest, taking an entire page to diagram each play.

A triumphant return to Chicago

In mid-November, 1938, Pacific played its first-ever intersectional game when they traveled back to Chicago to take on the University of Chicago Maroons. The trip was definitely not a luxurious vacation for a squad that had already clinched their conference title; for the entire team was assigned to one non-air conditioned tourist sleeper car. They brought along only five footballs, one of which was almost new. Pacific's athletic director Robert L. Breeden also doubled as the squad's trainer.

Pacific's traveling party was met at Chicago's Dearborn Street station by Maroons' coach Clark Shaughnessy, U of C athletic director T. Nelson Metcalf and a contingent of old Chicago players. The press asked Stagg why Stella didn't make the trip and he replied, "She's a better coach than I'll ever be. She stayed behind to scout our next opponent." The sports writers thought he was kidding, but he was dead serious.

Rather than attend all sorts of functions paying him homage, Stagg, without any warning, hired a big bus and took the team on a sightseeing tour. He wanted them to see that there wasn't any difference between the Pacific Ocean and Lake Michigan (unless you have to go some place in a big boat), he wanted them to see many other good things about the Windy City; but especially, he wanted them to understand that he harbored no bitter feelings at all about the city of Chicago or the university he once coached. The tour lasted all the Friday afternoon before the game and afterwards, the players said they really enjoyed it.

The Pacific-Chicago game was Chicago's homecoming contest, and that Friday night, 1500 U of C students and alums gathered before a huge bonfire in the center of the university's quadrangle. Stagg was there and spoke to them, saying, "I have sorrowed in your defeats and I have rejoiced in your victories. If you win tomorrow, it will be all right. And if the College of the Pacific wins, it will, of course, be all right. My responsibility as a coach makes it my duty to do all I can to bring victory to my team. But my feelings will not be hurt, regardless of who wins the game. Yours are friendly faces. Mine is the same to you."

More festivities took place before the game. Gordon Erickson, composer of "Wave the Flag of Old Chicago", was there to personally direct the University of Chicago Marching Band in a musical chronology of Stagg's career on The Midway. Then, the band's big bass drum, largest in the world, boomed 41 times in tribute to the number of seasons Stagg coached the Maroons. During the halftime intermission, an old-fashioned football game was staged, with players dressed in 1892-style uniforms.

Both teams sat on the same side of the field, since the U of C wanted the Tigers to feel like welcomed guests.

Stagg sat hatless on a bench behind his substitutes, just like the old days. Not once did he get worked up to the point of rising to his feet. There was no rushing to buttonhole any of his boys coming out of the game, no whispering into the ears of substitutes as he sent them into the contest. It was their game to play, after all, and it was just a breeze for the Grand Old Man.

Pacific never let up for an instant on offense or defense and won, 32-0. It had been bright and sunshiny with mild temperatures almost the entire afternoon and it wasn't until fifteen minutes after the folks had headed home after the grandest homecoming for the Grand Old Man was over, that rain began to fall and November returned to The Midway.

Despite a 1 and 3 start, Pacific finished at 7-3 that year, their best record ever against a strictly intercollegiate schedule. They were known as the "Thirty Every Thursday Boys", since their last three games of their thirty-man squad -- all victories -- were Thursday contests. Pacific dominated that season's All-Far Western Conference selections, with Tigers chosen for nine of the eleven slots.

1939: The Year of Pacific's "Golden Tigers"

To commemorate Stagg's fiftieth season in coaching, Pacific called its 1939 team the "Golden Tigers" and they sported golden jerseys for the occasion. The highlight of that grid campaign was their upsetting Cal, 6 to 0. "That was the year I started regularly playing an end or a back out in a flanking position, 15 to 20 yards away from the line. Out of that, I evolved many original strategies," recalled Mr. Stagg.

"That offensive system was really just emerging that year. For a time, it didn't seem as if we were getting anywhere with it, and I doubted very much that we were on the right track. But Stella always encouraged me that we were. Each season from then on, she worked with me in modifying and correcting this system."

Yes it was a team effort by Amos Alonzo and Stella all the way. Those Golden Tigers of 1939 knew it and their captain, Hugh McWilliams, publicly announced it when he delivered a "Tribute to Mrs. Amos Alonzo Stagg" over local radio. Stella was confined to a hospital bed while the team was out of town and McWilliams couldn't make the trip because of an injury, so the station thought it might cheer her up to have one of the players tell her how much she meant to the Tigers. Pacific's football captain said in his speech over the air, "To those of you who have ever played football, may I ask you this?

"Have you ever been warming up on a Monday afternoon, running a couple of laps, ironing out the game bumps, when you are stopped by an interested older lady who asks you, 'How does it feel?' Now, that is a unique situation, and one that we have right here in our own back yard.

"Mrs. Stagg, I'm not attempting to convey the idea that you are a mother to us; if our mothers knew as much about us as you have written in your little red book, they would probably never have allowed us to leave home. Incidentally Mrs. Stagg, please destroy Page 6, Volume II, where you noted that, 'H. McWilliams centered the ball to the field judge instead of the left halfback in a big game.'

"It was not until we came to Pacific and played football surrounded by this wholesome atmosphere that we fully realized the possibility of developing into better men through the game of football."

Nineteen thirty-nine was also the year that the American Football Coaches Association established the "Amos Alonzo Stagg Award". This lifetime achievement award has since become football's highest honor and is conferred annually by the AFCA upon the individual, group or institution who has made outstanding contributions to the advancement of football.

Grambling's legendary coach Eddie Robinson was one of the recipients of this honor. In recalling the Grand Old Man, Coach Robinson said, "I met Mr. Stagg at a Chicago coaches' convention in 1964 when he was 101 years old. I was just awed by the man. Everybody there was battling to sit at his table, but he walked right by the table that had his place card on it, came over to the table I was sitting at and asked me, 'Is it all right if I sit here?'

"'Of course,' I said.

"All the while he was sitting there with me, he talked about how, 'Coaching football was the greatest profession of all,' and how, 'No man was too good to spend time coaching America's youth.' He emphasized that, 'Above all else, you've got to tell 'em the truth.'

"Just that brief time I spent with him was an inspiration for me during my entire coaching career."

Stagg went out of his way to spend time with Eddie Robinson because, even as his days dwindled, the Grand Old Man was always reaching out to pass along the torch.

1940: Pacific vs. Notre Dame

Pacific opened their 1940 season with the long-awaited game against Notre Dame. Stagg took a squad of only 28 players, 13 of whom had never played in a varsity game before, into South Bend, Indiana to face a Fighting Irish team ranked among the nation's best. Once again, Stella didn't make the long rail trip back to the midwest, since she was not quite a hundred percent after her lengthy illness. She listened to the game on the radio, then drove to Fresno to scout Fresno State. When she got home, she was too wide awake for bed; so she spent the rest of the night painting the bathroom.

Little Pacific shocked the football world by leading at the end of the first quarter, 7 to 0. Pacific's touchdown resulted from a masterfully executed 19-play, 67-yard drive in which the Tigers went 7 for 7 in passing. After the halftime ceremonies which featured a singing performance by Kate Smith, the Fighting Irish finally wore out the Tigers and won, 25 to 7. C.O.P. came up short on the scoreboard, but had survived with honor. As a matter of fact the Tigers' left end Willie Boyarsky performed so well that he was voted to Notre Dame's 1940 All-Opponent team.

When the story got out about Stagg having had the advantage of all those Notre Dame game films and Elmer Layden was asked about Waldorf's involvement, the Notre Dame coach just smiled a knowing smile and said, "I'm just glad Stagg's team gave my men a tough game that helped them get ready for a tough season. What Lynn Waldorf did was the fair thing to do." No one, however, bothered to ask how Waldorf got all the Notre Dame movies, but it was really easy for Pappy. He just went to his good friend Elmer Layden. Both of those coaches would do anything to help the Grand Old Man.

This was just one instance in which an opposing coach helped Stagg out when C.O.P. was outmanned. In 1941, Pacific took less than 30 men to face top-ranked S.M.U. in a "Rose Festival Classic" held at Tyler, Texas. Two weeks before the game, S.M.U.'s head coach Matty Bell wrote Stagg and included in his letter diagrams of the Mustangs' three offenses, then closed with, "If there is anything else please let me know." -- just another indication of the respect all coaches had for the Grand Old Man.

Keeping the game alive during World War II

With the onset of World War II, most male students were inducted into military service before the 1942 season and it appeared unlikely that Pacific could continue football. President Knoles told Stagg that the situation was impossible and that he had best call it quits for the time being; as had Stanford, Oregon and Santa Clara.

Stagg listened respectfully, thanked Knoles and then went out and got ready to play football as usual. He did, however, voluntarily reduce his salary from $5000 per year

173

to $3000. If he had called it quits, Pacific's great 1943 season would never have happened.

At first, it did not seem to be a wise decision. Pacific's war-riddled squad won but twice in 1942, and it was a rough year for all concerned. C.O.P. student Boyd Thompson was asked to perform double duty as manager and trainer. After a very challenging year, the Grand Old Man recognized Thompson's contribution in a letter:

Dear Boyd;

It has been on my mind to express my appreciation to you of the manner in which you handled the very difficult double duties last fall of the club house and, later, the training job.

You won my sincere admiration by your good humor, your even temper, your resourcefulness, your intelligence, your faithfulness and your good judgment under difficult and rather trying circumstances. If you ever are in need of a recommendation from me, I shall be glad to give it.

"Later when I went into the Navy, I was assigned to Bainbridge Naval Station," recalled Thompson, "and I took Mr. Stagg's letter to the commanding officer. He took one look at it and assigned me immediately to be the trainer for Bainbridge's unbeaten service football team -- which had Paul 'Bear' Bryant as one of the coaches -- without having to tape one ankle as proof of my qualifications."

The 1943 Tigers: The most talented team Stagg ever coached

Stanford's wartime hiatus from football gave Pacific an opportunity to schedule California, U.C.L.A., Southern Cal and several powerful service teams, but the question remained: Where could the Grand Old Man find players that could win against the best. The answer came when the Navy selected C.O.P. as a training site for Naval and Marine officers. This brought in a tremendous group of football players who had gained experience at St. Mary's, Santa Clara, San Francisco and a half-dozen other colleges. "Uncle Sam furnished me with the best material that I ever worked with," Stagg said. "All the while they were going through boot camp, so we had just one hour for daily practice; but the players were in such superb condition and had so much know-how, that all I had to do was to teach them the plays, the strategies and the particular defense I wanted used for each game. I was able to use a new system of offense I had been working on. It was the easiest season I ever coached."

The two most prominent names on the squad were tackle Art McCaffray and halfback Johnny "Presto" Podesto from Modesto, who previously played at St. Mary's. Podesto had carved out a reputation as a passer for St. Mary's Gallopin' Gaels in 1942 with his 288-yard performance against Loyola of Los Angeles.

Stagg hired Larry "Sharkey" Siemering as his assistant in 1942, a young coach with impressive credentials. He was born in Lodi, California and became one of the greatest athletes ever produced by the San

Joaquin Valley area. Larry was a high school football star, then played three years at the University of San Francisco and was good enough to appear in both the East-West Shrine Game and the College All-Star Game; playing 58 minutes in both contests. Not only that, he was also expert at golf (winning a tournament at the age of 80 by shooting a 69), tennis, hunting and handball.

After two seasons with the NFL's Redskins, Siemering began his coaching career at Manteca High School, where he won three conference championships in four years. A year as head coach at Stockton High followed, where he was 10-0 and won another championship. Then, he spent a year as head coach at Stockton College and went 8-1, winning the league crown. Throughout his years coaching high school and junior college football, Siemering lost no more than one game in any one season; but because he came up through the ranks, Siemering had the respect of every high school and junior college coach in the region, any one of whom would try to help him if he asked.

The 1943 Pacific squad was a diverse group and, since none of them had any previous experience with Mr. Stagg's brand-new offense, it was difficult for some of the players to master their assignments. Halfback Jack Verutti had problems with the timing needed to correctly execute the question mark-shaped motion required of the Pedinger play. Finally in exasperation, Stagg shouted: "Count your steps, Verutti! Can't you count? It's just like music. You can dance. You have rhythm, don't you? Do you know the song, 'Yankee Doodle'?"

"Yes, Mr. Stagg."

"Well then, sing 'Yankee Doodle' to yourself while running the Pedinger and it will help you remember your steps."

Verutti began singing the ditty when he went in motion, and it worked beautifully. He would even sing it aloud while playing in games, and this earned him the nickname "Count" Verutti.

Pacific opened their '43 season against a veteran Alameda Coast Guard team in Kezar Stadium. The game was tied, 7 to 7, until, with only a minute and forty-five seconds left, John Podesto from Modesto whipped a touchdown pass to Carl Lueder, who dragged Coast Guardsman Gonzales Morales with him into the end zone, and Pacific won, 14-7.

It was the start of Podesto's six-game rampage. He threw a touchdown in each of those games, led the team in rushing yardage and did all the punting. The victory over Alameda Coast Guard set a pattern, because, in four out their next five games, Pacific had to come from behind or break a tie in the fourth quarter in order to win.

A rugged, experienced St. Mary's Pre-Flight squad came next. The Pre-Flighters led, 7 to 6, with only six minutes left to play when Lueder intercepted a pass and raced 65 yards for a touchdown, and Pacific won again. Pacific was favored the following week when they traveled south to face U.C.L.A.. In the huge Los Angeles Coliseum, the Bruins proved to be unexpectedly tough and the fourth quarter found Pacific in the hole again, at 7 to 6. Stagg's men, however, blazed for two touchdowns and won going away, 19 to 7. The next week it was California in Berkeley. The Bears were rated too strong for Pacific, but the Tigers knew better. "I'm tired of this last-minute stuff," grumbled Art McCaffray. "Let's get ahead in this game and stay there." Pacific led 12 to 0 at halftime, holding California without a first down and for minus yardage. The game ended as another close call, 12-6. The contest went down to the final seconds, when the Golden Bears failed to tie the score by missing on a touchdown pass by mere inches. The next week, Pacific had risen to tenth in the Associated Press poll.

Pacific's rooters were prepared for the worst when Stagg sent his team against Del Monte Pre-Flight, a game played to 11,090 -- Baxter Stadium's largest crowd ever. Del Monte had such stars as Len Eshmont of Fordham (later the 49ers) and Paul Christman of Missouri (the quarterback on the 1947 world championship Chicago Cardinals team). Pacific fell behind, as usual; then in the fourth quarter, Johnny Podesto fired a pass over Eshmont to Jack Hurley for a 37-yard touchdown which made it a 16 to 7 win for Pacific. Pacific now jumped to sixth in the A.P. rankings.

"I will never forget that Del Monte game," said Jack Verutti, "a clean, hard-fought, inspiring game despite the horrendous odds. And I'll never forget when we finally won and then carried Mr. Stagg off the field in a blaze of glory. As we carried him off the field and the crowd cheered him, I looked up at his amazed and slightly bewildered face, and tears were running down his cheeks. I thought to myself, 'What a privilege it is to carry on my shoulders the greatest coach in the world at the peak of his brilliant career.'"

Shortly after that in Pacific's dressing room, the *San Francisco Examiner's* Prescott Sullivan asked the Grand Old Man how he was going to celebrate. Stagg replied, "I'm going home and eat some figs."

That brought Pacific to its fiercest test of their 1943 campaign -- against U.S.C. The game had been scheduled at the last minute when a cancellation left Southern Cal with a home date to fill, and it would mean a second trip to the L.A. Coliseum that year; this time before 70,000 spectators -- the largest crowd to ever see a Stagg team play. Most of them wanted to see Pacific win, for the Grand Old Man's sake. By this time Pacific had fans pulling for them all over the country and the game was broadcast coast-to-coast by NBC's Bill Stern. Due to wartime travel restrictions, the 1944 Rose Bowl would have to match two west coast teams, so Pacific had been notified that, if they stayed on their unbeaten course, they would be invited to play the P.C.C. Champion in Pasadena's New Year's Day Classic.

It was apparent from the game's earliest moments that it would be tightly contested, and the first quarter ended without a score. Things began to heat up in the second stanza, especially after the Trojans drove to a fourth and six at Pacific's eight-yard line. Mickey McCardle fired a pass, but his receiver juggled the ball in the end zone and Pacific took over on their eight.

On third and five from his thirteen, Podesto broke loose for 52 yards and it was only Mickey McCardle's saving tackle that prevented a C.O.P. score. On the very next snap, Podesto threw a pass to Joe Ferem. Ferem caught the ball in stride at the SC 12-yard line, took a quick peek for an open path to the end zone, then looked for help from a blocker.

Years later in recalling that critical moment of the contest, Pacific end Jack Hurley said, "I was coming across to block Mickey McCardle, who was playing defensive halfback. He was to the inside of me and I was trying to take him down with my shoulder. At the last instant, he turned so that his back was toward me and tried to set me up so that it looked like I was clipping him. This was common practice back then.

"Later on, we wound up serving in the military together and became good friends. He told me one time, 'It was the greatest turning move I made all that season.'"

Meanwhile, Ferem sailed into the end zone for a 36-yard touchdown reception and the first score of the afternoon...then, suddenly, the action stopped when the referee blew his whistle. The referee ruled that Hurley had clipped McCardle and that Pacific's touchdown didn't count. It was plainly seen by everyone in the sold-out stadium, however, that the "whistle tooter" had blown the call.

The game raged on, still scoreless; then in the third quarter, Pacific suffered a series of injuries which hobbled their effort. Even Podesto went down for the first time that season. Still, Pacific held U.S.C. out of the end zone until the Trojans finally manufactured a fourth quarter touchdown pass. But the Tigers' Frank Holmes brought the crowd to its feet by returning the ensuing kickoff 95 yards for a TD that appeared to have tied the game, and with a converted PAT would have put Pacific back in front. Unfortunately, the referee wiped out another C.O.P.

touchdown by ruling Holmes had stepped out of bounds 47 yards from paydirt. USC's slim lead held up and the Trojans won, 6-0.

When the reporters asked the Grand Old Man about the C.O.P. touchdown which had been denied, he responded, "I didn't see the play in which the Pacific touchdown was called back for a clipping penalty. My boys jumped up and obstructed my view. Naturally, my boys were greatly put out when the officials called it back. Many of the fans were evidently also in disapproval, since I never heard so much booing in my life. If the Trojans feel that the official's decision was right, then I am satisfied they won the game fairly and squarely. On the other hand, if they feel the decision was wrong, it would be a very fine, commendable act of sportsmanship to ask for a replay of the game at some future date."

Pacific suffered their first loss of the season and was kept from the Rose Bowl -- all because of two questionable calls by the same official. It was a disappointing loss, not just for Pacific, but for all of Stockton to bear. Very few, however, were aware of the whole story. It was finally revealed nearly six years later when Tully Knoles addressed the American Football Coaches Association. "I should have been seated up in the stands," said Knoles, "but I was standing right there on the sidelines and I said something very profusely when the referee made that call on Hurley and Mr. Stagg pulled me back and he said,'You know, the referee has made his decision and that has got to stand.' Then I said, 'All right, if you say so.'

"Well, what is the future of that? That man who made the call came to referee that game in an Army uniform and changed to the referee's uniform for the game. After the game, he went back to the Army uniform. Eighteen months after that, he was arrested in the Army for embezzlement and I was amazed when they exhibited his bank balance and the prosecuting attorney showed his salary in the Army back through a period years, and they asked him how he ever got such an accumulation of money on a salary of that sort. He said, 'Betting on horse races and football games.'"

The referee in question was Tom Wilcox. He had conspired with the Bugsy Siegel-Mickey Cohen mob to make sure that USC won their important football game with Pacific that had generated huge wagering. Wilcox went to prison for embezzlement, but no one was ever prosecuted for fixing the football game.

Pacific finished out their 1943 schedule with victories over St. Mary's and Yuma Air Base, then were approached to play a post-season contest, with the gate receipts going to charity, against power-laden March Field in the Los Angeles Coliseum. The Fourth Air Force installation based in Riverside included such players as former Oklahoma star "Indian Jack" Jacobs and former U.C.L.A. star end Woody Strode on their roster. Unfortunately, due to circumstances beyond anyone's control, Pacific was hopelessly out-manned, since most of their squad was transferred to Parris Island a week before the game. Pacific's Tigers fought gamely, but lost, 20-0. They were then offered a bid to play in Lodi, California's Grape Bowl game, but the depleted team voted against accepting the invitation.

Despite the disappointing end to their season, the Tigers celebrated two of their players receiving national honors. Art McCaffray was picked for Grantland Rice's All-American team, the first Pacific player to be so honored, and John Podesto was chosen for Bill Stern's "Look Magazine All-American" list. The most stunning news, though, was the Football Writers Association voting Mr.Stagg "Football's Man of the Year" and the AFCA naming him "Coach of the Year" for the first time in his life -- at the age of 81.

Bill Schroeder, managing director of the Helms Athletic Foundation, vividly remembered the evening after the March Field game. "While we were having dinner, someone from CBS brought a wire report to me, noting that Coach Stagg had just been chosen College Football Coach of the Year," said Schroeder. "Just think of it! After over 50 years of coaching, Mr. Stagg still had enough on the ball to be named Coach of the Year. No coach, so long in years, had ever been accorded such an honor.

"I stood up and made the announcement, reading the wire report, then I called upon Mr. Stagg for a few comments. With tears streaming down his face, Mr. Stagg accepted the honor lightly, but said, 'All of the boys of this fine College of the Pacific team were the ones who were responsible for my having been chosen Coach of the Year.'

"Then, Presto Johnston, Pacific's team captain, immediately arose to his feet and, with tears streaming down his face, said, 'No, Mr. Stagg, you were the one who made us the fine team which we were this year. We were not responsible for you having been chosen Coach of the Year. It is your own honor!'

"All of this provided one of the most dramatic scenes which I have ever witnessed in the field of sports. It was my greatest sports thrill.

"I also recall one day, while Mr. and Mrs. Stagg were in Los Angeles, they walked into Helms Hall and told us they had come out to see us. I asked Mr. Stagg how they had made the trip to Helms Hall from downtown Los Angeles. He casually remarked that they rode out on the street car. I can assure you that we provided transportation for Mr. and Mrs. Stagg back to Los Angeles after they had made a tour of our sports shrine.

"I couldn't imagine any other famous and distinguished coach making a trip all the way out to Helms Hall from downtown Los Angeles on a street car to visit our sports shrine. Any other coach would have first called us and possibly asked if transportation might be provided...but not the Staggs -- who have never desired to inconvenience anyone.

"Needless to say, Mr. Stagg was elected to our Helms Athletic Hall of Fame as part of our original group of inductees in 1948; along with the likes of Baron Pierre de Coubertin, Walter Camp, Connie Mack and others, as one of the world's foremost contributors to sports.

"College football has never known a greater coach, nor a greater leader of men."

The courageous Pacific squads of 1944-1945: Battling against all odds

March 7, 1944, Arbor Day, was proclaimed "Amos Alonzo Stagg Day" by the mayor of Stockton and a Sequoia Gigantea was planted on the College of the Pacific campus in honor of the Grand Old Man. Mr. Stagg was grateful for all the good wishes and he needed everything he could get to sustain him during the 1944 football season; because that season was as difficult as the 1943 campaign had been exhilarating.

"Due to our success in 1943, we inherited a horrendous 1944 schedule," recalled Boyd Thompson. "C.O.P. was outmanned in most of the games and didn't win many; but we had some memorable moments.

"Jim 'Suds' Lyons was a lineman on that team, and, of course, we called him 'Suds' because he really loved that beer. He had come to Pacific on a track scholarship, went into the service, then got out of the service early due to a medical discharge.

"During one of those 1944 games, Suds made the mistake of intercepting a pass on his own two-yard line with superb downfield interference in front of him and a clear track to the end zone. A couple of players said later that they blocked twice for him on this same play.

"Lyons took off with the ball for all he was worth, but, not being in peak condition for one reason or another, he was totally spent by the time he reached the opponent's ten-yard line and literally collapsed face down on the turf.

"Mr. Stagg, at first, was concerned that there might've been something seriously wrong with Lyons, so he trotted out to Suds' prostrate form and asked: 'Jim, Jim. Are you all right?'

"Suds rolled over, looked at Mr. Stagg and answered, 'I'm okay. I just ran out of gas.'

"Mr. Stagg deadpanned, 'I don't think there was too much in your tank to begin with.'"

Pacific had to play their entire 1944 schedule extremely shorthanded. They won only three out eleven games, but were never disgraced. The Tigers took on USC in the L.A. Coliseum with only 19 men on the squad, and hung tough before losing, 18-6, to a Trojan team that went on to rout Tennessee by 25-0 in that year's Rose Bowl.

185

C.O.P.'s fortunes sunk even lower in 1945, when circumstances forced them to field a 17-man squad, with a line averaging only 177 pounds per man and a backfield averaging 161. Despite the hopelessness of the situation, the Tigers still managed a 7-7 tie with Santa Barbara Air Base and close losses to Stockton Air Base (12-6) and Camp Beale (13-7).

Things grew even more desperate that November when the semester ended and the Navy V-12 trainees received orders to transfer. That left Pacific with only six players and it took eight volunteers from the student body to bring the squad up to fourteen. The Tigers played the Albany Navy "Beachbusters" and narrowly lost, 18-13, but out gained their opponent in total offensive yardage.

There was no let up in bad breaks, though, and two of Pacific's players were injured in the game with the Beachbusters; so C.O.P. was forced to play a Thanksgiving Day contest with Fresno State using only twelve players. Amazingly, Pacific managed to hang in and, in the late stages of the contest, Jean Ridley caught a pass for a first down on Fresno's 12-yard line. That flicker of hope was extinguished, though, when Pacific turned the ball over on downs and lost, 16-0. The Tigers season record was 0-10-1, but the entire shorthanded squad deserved medals for finishing their eleven-game schedule.

Getting back to normal after the war

With the war ending, many of Pacific's players married and began raising families. "Mr. Stagg always kept in touch with his players for years after they finished school," recalled Jim Turner, a tackle at Pacific and

California and a five-time "All-Coast" selection, "especially when their children were born. Then he would send the new parents a check for one dollar to use in opening a savings account for their child.

"The problem was they would use his signed checks as keepsakes and nobody was cashing the checks. One day, I got a letter from Mr. Stagg saying that he was trying to balance his bank account and asking me to please cash his check and offering to send the canceled check back to me."

"It didn't matter," added Boyd Thompson. "Very few of those checks were ever cashed."

After the tumult and shouting of V. J. Day celebrations faded into the background, the nation's main concern became "getting back to normal"; but the C.O.P. Bengals would never return to the way things had been before, since they were on course toward a golden horizon.

STOCKTON EMERGES AS THE "FOOTBALL CITY OF THE WEST"

Pacific's enrollment was swelled in 1946 by the presence of World War II vets, and more than doubled to 1,137. This meant more candidates for the football team, but a new set of challenges appeared.

"In many ways 1946 was the toughest year Mr. Stagg ever faced in his coaching career," said Boyd Thompson. "The war vets who came out for football at Pacific were young men who had grown up in a hurry while in service, but many of them had acquired bad habits in the process. Mr. Stagg wasn't used to the lack of discipline shown by some of the players.

"Another problem was that, because of the length of time required for war vets to be discharged, there weren't enough C.O.P. football alums around in the spring of '46 for an alumni squad to play the varsity in the traditional game that ended spring practice. So, Mr. Stagg decided to suit me up.

"I managed to get the equipment on properly and to walk onto the field without tripping over myself, but a problem cropped up while I was playing left defensive halfback.

"The ball carrier ran wide to his left, which was to the right of me and on the other side of the field. I should have started running in that direction and try to chase him down; but I failed to do that and just stood there. Along came somebody running at full throttle and they blindsided me. I was laid out and I felt like I had been hit by a truck. Mr. Stagg came over to me and, after he determined that I was all right, said, 'Boyd, you just learned a very important lesson: Don't ever just stand around on a football field; keep moving and do something. Even if you're not sure what to do, do something. Otherwise, you could get clobbered.'

"I used this story many times, whenever I addressed groups of physicians during my career as lobbyist for a medical association, as an example of not allowing yourself to become locked into the status quo."

"At the start of fall practices," recalled Mr. Stagg, "we had entirely too small of a carryover of first-stringers from spring practice and hardly any of our lettermen were prospective starters. Even though we had a large roster, three-fourths of the candidates were new to my system of play; and most of our starters came from this group with no previous instruction from me."

Among the influx of freshmen was 5' 7" 165-pound quarterback Eddie LeBaron. He had grown up on a big farm near Oakdale, California. LeBaron was extremely bright and, as Larry Siemering recalled, "was playing varsity football at Oakdale High when he was twelve years old, also starred in basketball and track, and entered college at the age of 15. After seeing him play a single wing tailback and, with his punting and passing ability, Mr. Stagg was reminded of T.C.U.'s great Davey O'Brien."

Eddie LeBaron's infatuation with football came early. When he was four, an uncle who had played at St. Mary's gave him a football; and he would spend hours kicking and throwing the ball in the fields surrounding his parents home. He also took the ball to a nearby school, where he would play with the older kids during recess. His athletic and social abilities allowed him to start first grade at the age of five, and he jumped to third grade the following year, at the age of six, when there weren't enough kids to fill a second grade class.

LeBaron stated, "I was twelve and on the varsity that first year, but I only played with the junior varsity squad that played one or two games. After that year, my age was suddenly listed as fifteen on the roster; and I stayed fifteen for three years. I really grew up quickly.

"I don't think people cared about someone younger playing in those days. But I do know that they didn't want kids who were a lot older on the teams."

Even with all the experience he had for his young age, though, LeBaron's college career got off to a rocky start. "An attack of appendicitis prevented his calling the signals and doing the passing in our first game," said Stagg, "which was against the University of Oregon. They beat us, 7 to 6." Pacific won their next three games before embarking on a two-game, eleven-day excursion, and, this time, Stella made the trip.

Since it was common knowledge that 1946 would be Stagg's last year as Pacific's head coach; Northwestern invited C.O.P. to play in Evanston, Illinois that year, with the game tied into a tribute to the Grand Old Man by the Big Ten. The "eastward expedition" began with a Saturday night game at Tucson against the University of Arizona on October 19th. The Tigers left Stockton on Friday morning, October 18th. "Before the train had reached Bakersfield, though," said Boyd Thompson, "Mr. Stagg caught 'Eggs' Alvieri smoking while sitting in the lounge car. He gave him bus fare, had him put off the train and sent back to Stockton.   We arrived in Tucson at 10:45 A.M. the morning of the 19th.   After the game, won by Arizona, 47-13, we continued on by train to El Paso, Texas and stayed there until Tuesday night, October 22nd.

"C.O.P. took up the top floor of our hotel in El Paso. Several players were assigned to each room and slept in bunk beds, just like in the service.   One night, two of the players -- Jim Boyd and Ed Cathcart -- snuck out of the hotel and crossed the bridge into Juarez, Mexico.   They made it back into their rooms undetected, but they hadn't been in their bunks for more than a couple of hours, when Stagg walked in, blew his whistle, saying, 'All right, everybody up!   It's time for breakfast.   We're going to see the Carlsbad Caverns.'   He often took his teams on such tours during road trips because he thought the boys would really enjoy it.   In the case of Boyd and Cathcart, though, it was the last thing in the world they wanted to be doing. Mr. Stagg, however, never found out about their going to Juarez."

The train trip from El Paso to Chicago took 37 hours and, after playing Northwestern on October 26th, the Tigers wouldn't be back in Stockton until Tuesday, October 29th.
The idea of "going home" to play in Big Ten country really got the Grand Old Man pumped and Pacific's 84-year-old, white-haired coached startled NU's home crowd as he ran onto the field leading his Pacific Tigers into battle.   Meanwhile in the NU dressing room, Pappy Waldorf told his Wildcats, "After you knock 'em down, offer 'em a hand and help pick 'em up.   Do that for the Grand Old Man."

Northwestern's talented, resilient squad of war vets destined to be 1949 Rose Bowl champs held a 20-0 lead in the waning moments of the first half, when Eddie LeBaron intercepted a pass at his own five-yard line, then lateraled to Wayne Hardin, who caught the ball at Pacific's two. Hardin raced down to NU's 35-yard line and was about to be tackled, when he lateraled to John Rohde and Rohde sprinted in for a touchdown that got the Tigers back into the game.

With a 20-6 lead at halftime, Waldorf wouldn't allow NU's first and second teams to take the field for the third quarter. He put his third and fourth-string players into the game and sent the first and second units to Northwestern's practice field to run signal drills while the scrubs finished the game. But the fireworks weren't over.

In the fourth quarter, the Wildcats' Tom Worthington fumbled and the ball was picked up by C.O.P.'s Collie Kidwell. LeBaron took advantage of the opportunity to connect with Bob Atkinson for a TD on the next-to-last play of the game. The final score was Northwestern 26, Pacific 13.

C.O.P. finished 1946 at 5-6 and in second place in the California Collegiate Athletic Association, but, because it was Mr. Stagg's last season, they were invited to play North Texas State in Houston's Optimist Bowl. On December 7, however, Stagg announced his retirement from C.O.P. and that he had accepted an offer to become "advisory coach" at Susquehanna University in Selinsgrove, Pennsylvania. The Optimist Bowl would be his last game as Pacific's head coach.

Events had come to a head after C.O.P. proposed that Stagg step aside from active coaching to a less strenuous post of "consultant in athletics". It seems the Old Man had been physically slowing down. His mind was still like a steel trap, but his body was no longer up to the physical demands of being a head coach all by himself. Stagg, however, decided that, even at age 84, he wasn't old enough to retire; and that he and his son Alonzo, Jr. could combine to do a first-rate coaching job. The arrangement would be for the father and son team to be equals in coaching status. The elder Stagg took the offense and Junior took the defense. In addition, Stella would scout upcoming opponents.

Like Stagg's last act at Chicago, his boys tried their hardest, but narrowly lost the Optimist Bowl, 14-13. Corpus Christi, Texas attorney Warren Phillips attended the game and later wrote Mr. Stagg: "The officiating was terrible. Your team out gained North Texas by 182 yards and the difference would have been almost double that if your team had been allowed to keep its gains. North Texas was lucky to intercept your team's pass and return it for a score and to complete a pass to get to your 39-yard line. From there to the end of the game, your boys did not actually give up a yard. After North Texas was thrown for a big loss, your team was penalized 15 yards; which the way they marked it off turned out to be 35 yards, and then you were penalized again. The other team was given eight times to score before they finally hit a receiver for a touchdown.

"My boy and three of his friends, all high school football players, were with me. They all agreed: 'The officials played a good game for North Texas.' It was not really a loss. Both you and Pacific made many friends and the poor calls were resented and regretted by the spectators."

The "Black Knights of the Calaveras"

College of the Pacific held a farewell dinner for Mr. Stagg on February 18, 1947 and the team presented him with a beautiful suitcase and a scroll signed by the thirty-seven-man squad. Stagg was replaced at Pacific by Larry Siemering, who almost from the very moment his head coaching career began created two innovations that changed the face of football: The "Belly Series" and the "Full Spinner".

The Belly Series was birthed while Siemering was attempting to teach defensive ends how to shut off the slant play and still be able to hold up end runs. Eddie LeBaron was playing quarterback and John Poulos was at fullback. LeBaron was to fake handing the ball the ball off to the 238-pound Poulos, then pitch it to a halfback for an end run. At the snap of the ball, LeBaron met Poulos a couple of yards deep into the backfield. He inserted the ball into Poulos' midsection, and then attempted to pull the ball back in order to toss it to the trailing halfback. Without realizing it, though, Poulos clamped down exceptionally hard on the ball. Eddie was unable to shake the ball loose, consequently he had to run a couple of steps alongside Poulos. About the moment that Eddie retracted the ball, Poulos was tackled by a defensive end. Eddie then tossed the ball to the trailing halfback, who flew down the field all alone. Few coaches would have recognized what had occurred, but Larry Siemering did. From that beginning, he developed and polished the Belly Series.

The spark that led to the Full Spinner, sometimes called the "Whirling Dervish", occurred in a hotel lobby while C.O.P. awaited a bus to go to the stadium for a game. LeBaron had a football and, while probably rehearsing a standard maneuver, added an improvised finishing touch that caught Siemering's eye. He then had LeBaron execute the same maneuver; a full 360-dgree turn in one continuous, rapid motion. This was developed into a play in which: as the ball was snapped, a halfback sliced over the center on a fake trap play; then, without any hesitation or break in movement, LeBaron continued his full turn. At the end of the full turn, he either tossed the ball to the fullback for an end run, or faked the toss. A third variation of the maneuver called for LeBaron to fake handoffs, but keep the ball to carry it himself or throw a forward pass.

In the first year with the new offense, 1947, Pacific enjoyed an 8-1 record, with their only loss coming at the hands of Santa Clara, 21-20. The Tigers played in two bowl games after that season; winning the first bowl victories in C.O.P. history, as they beat Utah State, 35-21, in Lodi's Grape Bowl and trounced Wichita, 26-14, in Fresno, California's Raisin Bowl. The following year, 1948, the Tigers' record was 7-1-1 (San Jose State upset Pacific, 14-7, in a notorious "quick whistle" game. Loyola of Los Angeles had played them to a 14-14 tie earlier that season.). The Tigers again appeared in the Grape Bowl, where they met Hardin-Simmons and played to a wild 35-35 tie.

C.O.P.'s 1947 and 1948 campaigns segued into 1949, when Pacific's senior-laden squad enjoyed one of the greatest seasons in college football history. They compiled a perfect 11-0 season, averaged 7.7 touchdowns per game, scoring 575 points. Defensively, the Tigers yielded only 66 points that year. To San Joaquin Valley football fans, they'll always be their "'49ers", since 18 of the 22 seniors hailed from within 100 miles of Stockton.

The star of the team was Eddie LeBaron, who was their best runner, passer, punter and pass defender; but it was a veteran team with outstanding players at every position. Twelve of their running backs averaged a combined 6.2 yards per carry, and they had a big strong line that was excellent on both offense and defense. Don "Tiny" Campora was their outstanding lineman. Legend had it that Mr. Stagg was driving along in the Lodi area and spotted Campora with each hand on a tree shaking walnuts loose. Roy Muehlberger, a starting defensive tackle on Cal's 1949 Rose Bowl team played against Campora and said of him: "'Tiny' was anything but. He was a mountain of suet outweighing me by a hundred pounds; and I was 210 pounds, which was good size for a defensive lineman then. I played against him on a muddy field, and if he had gotten any traction at all, he would've killed somebody. Facing him was like having a kitchen table in your way, and, to him, I was just a cricket jumping around on his back. When he plugged the hole, he really plugged it."

The Tigers' toughest test was their season-opener against an imposing University of San Francisco squad (nine players on that team went on to play in the NFL) at Lodi's Grape Bowl. The Tigers won, 7-6, but had the ball the ball on the Dons' one-foot line as the game ended. They limited U.S.F. to just 143 yards in total offense and held Hall-of-Famer Ollie Matson to only 25 yards in eight carries, with Eddie LeBaron making two open field tackles on Matson.

Pacific won their next five games by a combined score of 270 to 47, then faced San Jose State in San Jose's Spartan Stadium, before a stadium-record crowd of 19,335 -- 5,000 of whom were C.O.P. fans making the trek from Stockton. Pacific won, 45-7, to avenge their 1948 loss to the Spartans (an impressive score, considering that same San Jose State went on to beat Texas Tech, 20-14, in the Raisin Bowl).

By this point of the season, Pacific had finally gained national media attention and Eddie LeBaron was being mentioned for All-American honors. The Tigers continued on an unbeaten path, trouncing Utah, 45-6, followed by a 45-0 whitewashing of Fresno State. Then, two road contests remained, starting with Cal Poly - San Luis Obispo; Pacific's last game before the season's final Associated Press poll was taken. It was felt that if somehow the Tigers could score 500 points in ten games this would help their cause, as far as national rankings and a possible big time bowl bid were concerned. Amazingly, Pacific beat Cal Poly S.L.O., 88 to 0, giving them a season total of precisely 500 points. Six years before, Army's Black Knights of the Hudson were the first to crack college football's 500 Point Barrier; so, in 1949, Stockton could rightly claim to be the home of the "Black Knights of the Calaveras. The final AP poll saw 10-0 Pacific ranked tenth in the nation. Only three other teams were 10-0 -- Notre Dame ranked first, Oklahoma second and California third -- but Pacific's sports information director Carroll Doty reminded the media that Pacific was the only one holding membership in the 500 Point Club.

Pacific's final 1949 game was before a sellout crowd of 28,000 in Honolulu against the University of Hawaii. The Tigers won, 75-0, and were so far ahead that even Dave

Hayden got to play. He was the team manager in 1949, but had been a player in 1947 before suffering an injury. Pacific finished the regular season at 11-0; scoring 575 points and surrendering only 66.

The victory over Hawaii should not have been the last game of the 1949 season, but, unfortunately, it was. C.O.P. declined a bid to Fresno's Raisin Bowl and held out for a bid to one of the four major New Year's Day classics. By all rights, they should have played Paul "Bear" Bryant's University of Kentucky team in the Orange Bowl at Miami, Florida. Santa Clara, however, with a proven track record of Sugar Bowl appearances and having narrowly lost to Oklahoma, 28-21, possessed enough clout to successfully lobby that the Broncos would be a bigger draw that the Tigers; even though their record was 7-2-1 compared to Pacific's 11-0. Pacific's boosters, though, believed they had an ace up their sleeve.

"Lowell Berry was a tremendous supporter of our football program," recalled Larry Siemering. "He was a USC grad, but for some reason didn't like the Trojans, so, fortunately for us, he switched his allegiance to C.O.P.; even becoming a member of the Board of Regents. He had become extremely wealthy as a contractor and had the means which he thought would enable him to make football's hottest young coach of a nationally-ranked team an offer he couldn't refuse.

"Berry met with Oklahoma's Bud Wilkinson, laid $100,000 in cash on the table and told him that, if the Sooners played Pacific in a brand-new bowl game in San Francisco's Kezar Stadium on New Year's Day, the University of Oklahoma could keep the money as a guarantee. $100,000 was a huge payday for bowl games in those days.

"The game never came off, but, if it had, it would have been one they'd still be talking about."

Without a bowl game to go to, it all came to individual honors. At the conclusion of his four-year career at Pacific, Eddie LeBaron had completed 204 of 430 passes for 3,841 yards and a school-record 49 touchdowns (a mark which stood for 42 years).   He was chosen on three All-American lists -- INS, NEA and Deke Houlgate.   In addition, LeBaron was a unanimous All-Coast choice and also received the inaugural "Pop Warner Award" as the west's top senior football player.   Eddie's teammates John Rohde, Harry Kane and Don Campora were picked on at least one All-Coast team by the three major wire services.

The incessant debate of: "Who's best in the west?" still had not been resolved, though.   Pacific challenged Cal to a post-season game as a charity benefit, but, not surprisingly, the offer was refused.   When Eddie LeBaron's classmates learned that the *San Francisco Chronicle's* Bill Leiser had decided not to cast an All-American ballot for their hero, they mounted a "Hate Bill Leiser Week", hanged the sports writer in effigy and organized an automobile caravan of 600 students which traveled to San Francisco for a demonstration in front of the newspaper's offices.   Metropolitan sports writers around the country may not have known it, but LeBaron was definitely the people's choice in the San Joaquin Valley. Further proof of LeBaron's status was a float with a floral replica of "Honest Eddie" entered by the Stockton Chamber of Commerce in Pasadena's Tournament of Roses Parade.

LeBaron did get to play in the East-West Shrine Game on New Year's Eve. Don Campora also appeared in that game, and he and Eddie were the first two C.O.P. players to ever participate in that contest. Their West squad lost, 28-6, but LeBaron was the hit of the proceedings and was voted the Most Valuable Player. The *San Francisco Chronicle's* Will Connolly wrote: "The crowd felt sorry for LeBaron against those big guys when he made his first appearance midway in the opening quarter. Michigan's Wally Teninga had punted out of bounds on the West three-yard line and the team was in a tough spot.

"But the first crack out of the box, Eddie circled left end for six. Then he went up the middle for five, behind the blocking of Southern Methodist's Dick McKissack, who was his helper all afternoon.

"At this show of success, the crowd ceased to sympathize with LeBaron, and, instead, roared its appreciation. Whenever Eddie trotted off the field in his blue and gold armor, the people set up a clamor.

"LeBaron's performances were all the more remarkable in that he was operating from the double wingback formation, a system strange to him. At Pacific, he was a throwing T-quarterback. The little squirt, used affectionately, wasn't supposed to be much of a runner, but he swept the East ends and barged up the middle for substantial gains. All day, the West gained 151 yards on the ground, and LeBaron contributed 108."

LeBaron also played in the inaugural Senior Bowl Game -- the first college all-star game organized so that the players would be paid to play. It was held in Jacksonville, Florida on January 7, 1950 and matched the "Yankee All-Stars" against the "Rebel All-Stars" before a crowd of 20,000. The Rebels beat Eddie's Yankee team, 22-13, but

LeBaron played impressively and threw a 46-yard touchdown pass to Oklahoma's Jim Owens. Each member of the winning Rebel squad received $475, while the Yankee players took home $343 bucks apiece. The money LeBaron was paid in Jacksonville, however, turned out to be small change compared to what he'd be paid for his next pro game, a special contest arranged to match "Honest Eddie" against another top quarterback -- Bob "Mad Engineer" Celeri.

Celeri had played for Cal, the giant university whose emblem is on the state flag, led his team to the 1950 Rose Bowl and made several All-America lists. Celeri was another local hero and his hometown of Fort Bragg presented him with a brand-new 1950 Chevrolet convertible. When the college draft was held, the pros picked Eddie as their 122nd choice and Celeri 126th; too close to draw any conclusions. The Celeri-LeBaron debate went on and on and eventually sparked a game held on Sunday, February 12, 1950 -- an event that proved more lucrative for the participants than any play for pay game that season.

The promotion was the brainchild of former California halfback Ted Kenfield, along with Cal law students Jack Stearns and Bob Holcomb. The three Cal men co-promoted it with the Lodi Chamber of Commerce. It was held in Lodi's Grape Bowl and matched the "Celeri All-Stars", consisting of 22 former Cal players, against the "LeBaron All-Stars", 22 former C.O.P. gridders. Even though it was a true professional football contest, no stadium rental was charged because the people in the area wanted to assure that practically all of the money went to the players. The cash would be "graduation presents" to their local heroes. The public's response was overwhelming. Ticket demand was so great that a three-to-a-customer limit had to be invoked. Not only were all 20,800 seats sold a week ahead of time at $2.50 apiece, but thousands of standing room tickets were also sold, swelling the total attendance to 24,218. LeBaron and Celeri were each guaranteed $2,000 plus 10 percent of the gross and they each wound up pocketing $5,000. Every other player in the game was guaranteed $500 and wound up with $550. Cal defensive tackle Roy Muehlberger was one of the "Celeri All-Stars" and he put his money to good use, buying an engagement ring for Nancy, who he has been happily married to for over fifty years.

The promotion took the Bay Area by storm. The San Francisco 49ers pitched in by loaning the "Celeris" 22 full sets of uniforms. All the major newspapers in the area covered it. Officially, no member of the University of California or College of the Pacific athletic departments were involved, but Cal athletic director Brutus Hamilton, Pacific's head coach Larry Siemering and Governor Earl Warren were all there. Even the Grand Old Man was in attendance, and at halftime Stagg presented awards to the San Joaquin Valley Conference's all-league team. Among the missing, though, was Carl Franz, father of Cal's only three-time All-American Rod Franz. Roy Muehlberger explained when he said, "Rod Franz' father, out of principle, wouldn't go because he didn't see any good in pro football. It was the first time he ever missed one of his son's games."

It was discovered, unfortunately, that football in February doesn't make for firm footing. The field was very sloppy and the game turned into a mud bath. Bruce

Orvis scored a touchdown for the "LeBarons" from one yard out and Wayne Hardin kicked the extra point. Later, Billy Montagne scored for the "Celeris", also from a yard out; but Cal's record-setting placekicker Jim "Truck" Cullom, shockingly, failed on his PAT attempt. So, the LeBarons edged the Celeris, 7-6. It made the locals very happy and they gleefully chanted: "We beat the Rose Bowlers!!"

The event was such a smashing success that Kenfield was contacted by other promoters who wanted to stage a series of LeBaron Vs. Celeri clashes in San Francisco's Kezar Stadium, the L.A. Coliseum and in Hawaii. Unfortunately, the players couldn't take enough time away from their studies to pursue those additional opportunities.

The biggest thing to come out of the promotion, though, was that it encouraged Lowell Berry to mount a drive for funds through sale of "script" redeemable for football tickets over a ten-year period to be used for construction of a stadium on the land Amos Alonzo Stagg donated to the school. The new stadium would be a memorial to those who had served in World War II. Things moved quickly, and within two months, sale of the script had netted $165,000. Groundbreaking ceremonies were held on April 20, 1950 and, just six months later, the new Pacific Memorial Stadium -- with a capacity of 36,000 and room to expand to 44,000 -- hosted C.O.P.'s homecoming game.

Some 32,000 spectators listened to speeches by such dignitaries as Governor Earl Warren and film star Dick Powell, then watched an exciting game. Unfortunately, Loyola of Los Angeles put a damper on the proceedings by edging Pacific, 35-33. A year later, an all-time stadium attendance record was set when 41,607 witnessed the Tigers' game against the great University of San Francisco team featuring Ollie Matson and Gino Marchetti. Again the Tigers suffered a defeat before a large home crowd, this time by a score of 47 to 14.

"John Peri was the sports editor of the *Stockton Record* then," recalled former Stockton College and C.O.P. player Don Gwaltney, "and he was always trying to instigate contests between Stockton athletes and athletes from the Bay Area. Ollie Matson and Pacific's Eddie Macon had competed against each other during the spring and summer of 1951 for a spot on the U.S. Olympic team in the 440-yard dash. Well, Peri played this angle up in his pregame writeups when U.S.F. played Pacific.

"Pacific was hanging right in there until Matson broke loose for a 90-yard touchdown run late in the game. Macon was right with him, almost stride for stride, all the way down the field. He couldn't get his arms around Ollie, so he made a diving effort to tackle him near the end of the run. Eddie was so close to him that he unintentionally bit Matson's heel and lost some teeth in the process. Macon went on to become the first African-American to play for the Chicago Bears.

"All of this is important because it shows how important Mr. Stagg was not just to Pacific, but to all of Stockton. None of it -- the stadium, the big crowds -- would have happened if it wasn't for the Grand Old Man.

"When he first came to Pacific, it was a tiny college hanging on by its fingernails to keep the doors open and barely able to put a 30-man squad on the field. At the end of his years as head coach, Pacific had deep, talented teams that could take on the nation's best, and, from 1950 to 1954,

Pacific sent more players to the pros than any other school -- 36 were drafted by the NFL."

On October 15, 1988, Pacific Memorial Stadium was renamed "Amos Alonzo Stagg Memorial Stadium". President Ronald Reagan sent the university a congratulatory letter in which he wrote: "Fans everywhere, including this one, can testify that Amos Alonzo Stagg's squads were topnotch, from Stockton to South Bend and all across our land. Coach Stagg created a legacy of character, skill, devotion and accomplishment."

Thirteen players from Pacific's 44-man 1949 roster were drafted by NFL teams, including Eddie LeBaron, who was chosen by the Washington Redskins. With the escalation of the Korean War during the summer of 1950, though, LeBaron was called to active duty in the United States Marine Corps. He accepted a commission in August and, while on leave, led the College All-Stars to a 17-7 upset over the Philadelphia Eagles (One of the All-Stars' two touchdowns was a 35-yard LeBaron scoring strike to North Carolina's Charlie "Choo Choo" Justice, then Eddie narrowly lost out to Justice in the MVP balloting.) "Bobby Dodd was the head coach of the All-Stars that year," said former Tiger John Rohde, who later became Pacific's head coach. "He learned the Belly Series from LeBaron at the All-Stars' training camp, then he took it back to Georgia Tech with him and used it to win two SEC titles and six straight bowl games." After the game in Chicago, LeBaron checked into the Redskins' training camp long enough for two preseason contests before his leave ended.

The Marines assigned him to the Quantico Marine Corps Schools in Virginia, which had a highly regarded service football team; and he arrived barely in time to suit up for the Quantico Leathernecks against Xavier University of Cincinnati, Ohio. The *Quantico Sentry* reported: "His gridiron debut was far from auspicious. He and several other starters had just reported and had little time for practice. Xavier bombed the locals, 34-13, with the Musketeers line granting little time for LeBaron's patented double-spin handoffs."

But Quantico was not to lose again until December 2, 1950, when they played College of the Pacific in the post-season Valley Bowl at Stockton. Quantico held a 14-9 halftime lead, but Pacific came back to win handily, 37-14. "We'd had a good season and wanted to play one more time," said Pacific lineman Burt Delavan, "but that game really burned us up. Here we are playing at home and all of our fans are chanting: 'Eddie! Eddie! Eddie!', cheering on our opponent.

"Pat Ribiero, our 6'6" defensive tackle, had enough of it and was singing a version of the Marine Corps Hymn the whole game: 'From the Halls of Montezuma to the shores of Tripoli, you are here to get your butts kicked, try to run the ball at me.'

"This all happened in the days before facemasks and, at one point, I broke through and nailed LeBaron, hitting him in the face. Later, he said to me: 'I'm disappointed in you.'"

Even with Quantico's getting ambushed in Stockton, LeBaron was named "Service Football Player of the Year" by the Washington Touchdown Club. His first priority, however, was to serve his country, and the *Quantico Sentry* noted: "LeBaron was a Marine first and a football player second. Within five months, he was far removed from the adoring and cheering fans and serving as a platoon leader in Korea, where he was twice wounded and awarded the Bronze Star for heroism in combat."

After Korea, "Honest Eddie" became known as "The General of The NFL". In eleven seasons as an NFL quarterback LeBaron passed for 13,399 yards and was a four-time Pro Bowl selection. Though one of the league's smallest players, LeBaron was the toughest quarterback. The harder he was knocked to the ground, it seemed, the quicker he would bounce to his feet, pat a menacing pass rusher on the rump and tell him: "Nice hit, guy. Let's see you try it again." Former Redskins' trainer Warren Arial recalled: "Eddie spent a lot of time sitting in a whirlpool reading his law books." After earning his law degree, he went on to head the Atlanta Falcons for nearly a decade.

Stagg's years at Susquehanna

Meanwhile back in Pennsylvania, the Staggs were having an enjoyable time making football a family affair. These were years when Lon and Stella would be in Selinsgrove from August through Thanksgiving and spend the rest of the time in Stockton. Stagg later recalled, "During my six years at Susquehanna, I created a new system of offense which, along with the strong defensive play developed by my son, enabled this small college to win more than its share of games against uniformly larger colleges with superior manpower."

Football historian Jim Campbell wrote, "The presence of Stagg, Sr. was pretty heady stuff for a sleepy river town of 3,500. Edward R. Murrow brought a CBS-TV film crew to town to do a segment run on the network's 'See It Now' show. During the filming, Murrow asked Stagg, Sr., 'Do you think you'll ever make a good coach out of him (indicating the nearby Stagg, Jr.)?' With a full measure of fatherly pride, Stagg, Sr. answered Murrow, 'He's already a good coach.' Stagg, Sr. could have added that his son was also a fine gentleman."

Amos Alonzo Stagg, Jr. further explained the coaching situation when he stated, "I would not have asked my father to come to Susquehanna just to be a figurehead who really didn't do any coaching." Each could concentrate on their forte: the father on offense, the son on defense. Stella continued being a "super sleuth".

"We were getting on the bus to go to our first game of the season," recalled Jim Hazlett,who played center for Susquehanna during the Grand Old Man's years with the Crusaders, "and one of us asked 'Will Mrs. Stagg be making the trip?' Mr. Stagg replied, 'No, she'll be busy scouting Dickinson for me.'" Stella hadn't lost her keen eye for football and when she gave Lon her report, she stressed, "You can get a man behind their left defensive halfback. He's slow on covering." The following Saturday, with the score tied late in the final quarter, Susquehanna's quarterback fired a pass over the head of that same defender for the winning touchdown.

Jim Hazlett also recalled that, "Susquehanna was a Lutheran school and daily chapel was held in those days. Various members of the faculty or the administration would serve as moderators, but hardly any students would show up.   When Mr. Stagg served as moderator, though, everyone would make it a point to be there."

Aside from the football knowledge Stagg brought to Susquehanna's players and the celebrity status he brought to the school, the Grand Old Man brought even bigger, longer-lasting things to the campus. "The two men who were the biggest influences in my life were my father and Amos Alonzo Stagg," recalled former Susquehanna lineman Bob Pittello. "My father taught me discipline and Mr. Stagg gave me my philosophy of life."

Jim Hazlett further elaborated on this when he said. "Each football season began in the heat of August, would continue through September, October and end just before Thanksgiving.   As the weather grew colder, we'd often ask ourselves, 'What will Mr. Stagg be wearing at practice today?'   He'd start the season with a short-sleeve shirt, then would go to a shirt and sweater and would add more layers of clothing as the weather became colder.   At the start of each practice on cold days, Mrs. Stagg would always drive up, then walk over to Mr. Stagg and ask him, 'Lonnie, are you warm enough?   Could you use a heavier coat?'   He'd usually tell her, 'No, Stella.   I'm fine.'
    "It was also apparent that a wonderful relationship existed between Mr. Stagg and his son Amos Alonzo, Jr. During practices and meetings, Alonzo, Jr. never referred to his dad as 'Mr. Stagg' or 'Coach', but always 'Father'.
    "As a result of seeing these things on a daily basis during football season, Susquehanna's players were given examples of the devotion husbands and wives should have for each other; and by observing what went on between Mr. Stagg and Amos Alonzo, Jr., we could see what it meant to be a good father.   These were things we carried with us

through our lives and were gifts given to us simply because of the time Mr. and Mrs. Stagg spent at Susquehanna."

"Even with such a storied mentor as Amos Alonzo Stagg, Sr. to co-direct the team, Susquehanna had a roller coaster ride -- 4-1-2 in 1947, 2-6 in 1948, 1-7 in 1949," stated Jim Campbell. "But things were coming together. In 1950, the Staggs co-produced a 4-2-1 mark.

"Then in 1951, the small church-related college experienced its first undefeated *and* untied team -- 6-0." After the last game of that 6-0 season, the players carried the 88-year-old Grand Old Man off the field in celebration.

"The Staggs were together one more season, 1952," added Campbell. "It was a 4-3 year. After that, Stella became too ill to make the trip in from Stockton each fall, and Mr. Stagg was forced to resign his position."

The NCAA Football Records Manual credits Amos Alonzo Stagg with 314 wins, 199 losses and 35 ties lifetime; but the 21 wins he helped compile at Susquehanna were not included because official Susquehanna records at the time indicated that Stagg, Sr. was an "advisory coach," even though his son and players from those teams insisted that he was at the very least a co-coach. A movement to have the NCAA officially recognize the 21 victories was launched, but to no avail; since the unique father-son co-head coaching arrangement was too far removed in time for the NCAA to take action. So, the NCAA ruled against Susquehanna's appeal for the record change in 1981, and again in 1996. Paul Stagg's comment on this situation was, "Nobody should waste their time fighting to have any more wins added to my Dad's record. He himself would've considered that of no importance whatsoever."

Still it would be nice to have the feats of the Susquehanna Crusaders be officially part of the Grand Old Man's coaching ledger. The most significant statistic of Stagg's amazing career, though, is the number of games he coached. Even with today's eleven-game and twelve-game schedules, it remains a remarkable achievement to coach over 500 college football games.

The Grand Old Man's last hurrah

The end of the trips to Pennsylvania, though, did not mean the end of football for Stagg. He accepted an assistant coaching job at Stockton College, explaining, "I am fit and able and I refuse to become an idle nuisance. Besides, I must keep my promise to God to work with youths as long as I'm allowed to stay on this earth."

By that time, Stockton College embraced the final two years of high school, as well as the first two years of college. It had two football teams: One a high school unit, and the other a junior college squad. Stagg served as passing and punting coach for the two teams.

He was on the Mustangs' coaching staff from 1953 through 1959, working for three head coaches during that time span. At first, Earl Klapstein was Stockton College's head coach. Klapstein was from Lodi, California. He had played center in high school, but Stagg switched him to blocking back, and then converted him to tackle in 1943. Klapstein later played for the Pittsburgh Steelers and after he left Stockton College, one of his coaching stops was a season spent as chief scout and defensive line coach of the Green Bay Packers. Klapstein was succeeded by Don Hall, who was replaced by Stan Cramer.

The Grand Old Man would show up like clockwork, trot an entire lap around the practice field, then he would be ready to coach Stockton College's special teams. From 1955-58, the Mustangs won or shared four conference titles and scored victories in three bowl games. Don Hall credited Stagg with a share of the team's success when he said, "He was our punting coach. That may not sound like much, but Mr. Stagg had long ago devised a method of blocking for the punter which required only three men to handle five men rushing up the middle. This allowed seven of our men to run downfield and converge on the opposing punt returner. He also taught his unique method of punting: A 'rocker-step' style which was a 'two-step punt', with the punter actually taking only one step. This made it nearly impossible for any of our punts to be blocked. We gave up hardly any return yardage and kept our opponents from returning any punts for touchdowns; or even getting decent field position. Needless to say, this was a big part of our success.

"We did have one scary moment in 1954, when Mr. Stagg took a hard hit from a player during one of the practices."

"I was at left guard," recalled Don Gwaltney, "and Tom Mitchell was at right guard, with Romer Derr at center. Romer's father, incidentally, was governor of Alaska, which at the time still had not been granted statehood.

"Derr had his head down, waiting to snap the ball. Mr. Stagg didn't like something about the way we were lined up and began walking toward the line of scrimmage. I hollered: 'Romer, watch out!' With that, Derr snapped the ball, blew off the line with his head down and hit Mr.

Stagg right in the gut.   He knocked him flat on his back and sent his papers flying all over the place.

"Don Hall hollered, 'Jesus Christ!   You killed the Grand Old Man!' and ran out to where Stagg was laying."

"At first, I thought, 'Omigod, is he dead?', recalled Don Hall, "but he came to as I was running out to him.   He just laid there as I asked him, 'Do you want me to call an ambulance?'

"'No, I'm all right,' he said.   'I can tell if I've really been hurt or not.   Just help me get up and I'll rest a moment.   Really, I'm all right.   Finish your practice, coach.'   Then, he stood leaning against a goal post for the rest of the practice.

"The next day, though, Mr. Stagg called to tell me, 'I won't be at work.   I'm too stiff and sore from yesterday's practice.'"

"Four days later," added Don Gwaltney, "Mr. Stagg was back out running his lap, then coaching our punt unit.

"The day after the mishap, the *Stockton Record* ran a headline: 'Grand Old Man Run Over By Romer Derr'. The wire services picked up the story and it was carried all over the country, even in Alaska.   We found out people heard about it up there when Romer's father called him and said, 'For God's sake, son, I'm up for reelection and you had to run over the Grand Old Man!'"

The teammates' last years together in Stockton

The years went by, but were never lost.   At the time of Stagg's birth, a man was lucky to live past forty; so, as the Grand Old Man neared the age of ninety, he thanked the Lord for each new sunrise and did all he could to make each day a good one. The city of Stockton started a tradition of gala celebrations on the occasion of Mr. Stagg's ninetieth birthday, since, from that point on, each birthday could be his last. Stagg, however, tried to temper their enthusiasm when he quipped, "I may live forever, because very few people die after ninety."

The national media got caught up in the spirit and birthday greetings poured in from all over. Fred Long Farley, chairman of Pacific's Department of Ancient Languages, wrote a poem for the occasion.

TO AMOS ALONZO STAGG ON HIS NINETIETH BIRTHDAY ANNIVERSARY

Since Adam said "tomorrow" or "last year"
Man has a measuring-rod. He calls it "Time."
Thanks to stargazers' cry, "Moon in its prime!"
Our months are named and calendars appear.
But more than empty years, blessings adhere
To humankind, unmarked; blessings sublime
And luminous in man's uncertain climb;
And these are they which encompass man's career.

Now you, dear friend -- distinguished "grand old man" --
Have breasted four score years and ten. But you
Made of those years more than mere wondrous span.
You captured blessings weaker men pursue;
Coach, comrade, mentor, Christian, puritan.
And so we give this day our love anew.

Stockton celebrated Stagg's ninety-fifth birthday on August 16, 1957 with a luncheon at the Hotel Stockton and

Notre Dame's Frank Leahy as the guest speaker. The Grand Old Man took the occasion to talk about the home he and Stella had found there. He said, "Belonging! Belonging! It's a great thing to belong. It gets hold of your heart and your soul. There is nothing like it.

"All of us here belong to one another. It will always be that way.

"You treated us as one of your own. We came from Chicago, but you took us into your hearts, and we have called Stockton home ever since. We haven't wanted to move at any time.

"I don't know how long it will go on. I want to live long enough to look after Stella, and Stella wants to live long enough to look after me. We're in love with one another. That is sufficient."

That night, the Elks Valley High School All-Star Game was played in Lodi's Grape Bowl and Mr. Stagg served as honorary chairman of the event. He told the players at the kickoff luncheon. "Whatever thy hand findeth to do, do it with thy might -- Ecclesiastes 9:10. That Bible passage is my personal favorite. I put the meaning of it in my mind at an early age and have retained it all the way. Keep God in your minds all the time and you will be real men -- men with opinions, thoughts and actions.

"I can't be too grateful to God that I am here. 124 men graduated from Yale in 1888 and only three are alive; one of whom has spent the last three years in a hospital.

"Selection for this all-star game means certain responsibilities. It means you must be ready to make sacrifices. You must be cooperative and possess sustained enthusiasm to carry you through until the final whistle.

"However, this game is only a small part of life. You youngsters will have assignments throughout your life

-- be a man all the way. Don't be ashamed to get down on your knees to do a little work – I've had to do it, and so have all the rest of us."

Despite everything the doctors tried, though, they could not prevent Amos Alonzo Stagg's eyesight from growing dim; and that forced him from coaching in 1960. On September 16th of that year, he wrote Stockton College head coach Stan Cramer, "It is with deep regret that I will not be able to accept your invitation to come out for football practice this year. For the past 70 years, I have been a coach. At 98 years of age, it seems a good time to stop."

Though his infirmities prohibited his actually coaching, Mr. Stagg was still eager to share his hard-won knowledge with young coaches; and they were always welcome at his home on Stockton's Euclid Avenue. Iowa State's Clay Stapleton (Stapleton coached ISU's legendary 1959 "Dirty Thirty" team and has been inducted into the Iowa State Sports Hall of Fame) brought his entire staff to see the Grand Old Man when the Cyclones paid the Tigers a visit in November 1960. Mr. Stagg said to them, "Each of you must realize that, in the course of your careers, every one of you will be fired; but you are still part of the greatest profession of all; being a football coach.

"The ideals of every coach should be fair-mindedness, clean language and living, avoidance of politics and avoidance of graft. No man is too good to be an athletic coach for youth."

Lynn "Pappy" Waldorf, a coaching legend who learned from Stagg, captured the Grand Old Man's essence when he stated: "Mr. Stagg was in American football from its very beginnings and saw that the game matured into what it is today. No man made a greater contribution to football. Above all, though, he lived his life as the Sermon on the Mount; not as a dusty platitude, but as a joyous inspiration to man."

The Grand Old Man's one hundredth birthday was celebrated from coast to coast on August 16, 1962. A gala party was held for him in Stockton's Civic Auditorium, and California's Governor Pat Brown attended the affair. A three-foot-high birthday cake with one hundred candles was baked for the occasion.

The altruistic, humble coach of all coaches attended the festivities and when asked to speak said, "I never anticipated living to 100. I have lived my life day by day, and I'm surprised to be here."

Mr. Stagg received over 500 birthday cards and letters from well-wishers; as well as many telegrams, including one that arrived late at night. He had already gone to bed, so the telegram was in his mailbox the next morning. It read, "To all Americans who love their country, your emphasis on the moral and physical values of the vigorous life have been warmly appreciated." It was signed, "John F. Kennedy."

By the end of 1962, the Staggs' health had declined so that Amos Alonzo and Stella became permanent residents of the Hillhaven Convalescent Hospital in Stockton. In his last years, Stagg had grown tired and weary; he was losing his sight and was becoming feeble, and the same could be said for Stella. She was bedridden and it wasn't often that he could visit her in the women's part of their nursing home. Stella died during the summer of 1964 at the age of 88. She had a magnificent funeral, with the same six pall bearers her Lon would have; but no one told the Grand Old Man, for they knew it would break his heart.

They knew that he didn't want to die alone; that he wanted her by his side where he could reach out and hold her hand when he passed on. Whenever he asked if he could see her, they'd tell him he couldn't because she "wasn't up to it", she was "resting". He seemed to understand, because he never questioned them any further. But it was also apparent that it was just too painful to allow the thought that they weren't telling the truth to ever cross his mind. It all became very, very hard for him. Finally, less than a year later, angels came and took him to her.

Amos Alonzo Stagg's life ended on Wednesday, March 17, 1965; but it was not the end of his tale. The game he created has lived on, and each time a football game is played, another paragraph is added to his everlasting saga. His game of football is not the same as when he coached, and certainly not what it was when he played. There are more bowl games than ever before, even one named for the Grand Old Man -- the "Stagg Bowl" which decides college football's Division III championship. There's more pro football than ever, there's more money involved than ever before, and television is a huge part of the scene. Football is part of our nation's finest institutions of higher learning, yet it has become prime time entertainment geared to the most common denominator. But it is still based upon blocking and tackling, punting and placekicking, the forward pass and each player facing a moment of truth on every snap -- just as it has always been since Mr. Stagg started his game. For it to continue and to inspire generations to come -- to remain an everlasting investment in mankind -- it must face challenges brought to bear through societal changes. Now more than ever, it is critical for coaches to be less concerned with counting wins and dollars, and be totally committed to building virtues. In this way, the Grand Old Man's game will be forever honored... and his story will never end.